I USED TO KNOW THAT
HISTORY

I USED TO KNOW THAT
HISTORY

STUFF YOU FORGOT FROM SCHOOL

EMMA MARRIOTT

FOREWORD BY CAROLINE TAGGART

Michael O'Mara Books Limited

For Robin, and his uncanny ability to remember stuff.

This paperback edition first published in 2015

First published in Great Britain in 2010 by
Michael O'Mara Books Limited
9 Lion Yard
Tremadoc Road
London SW4 7NQ

A CIP catalogue record for this book is available from the British Library.

Papers used by Michael O'Mara Books Limited are natural,
recyclable products made from wood grown in sustainable
forests. The manufacturing processes conform to the
environmental regulations of the country of origin.

ISBN: 978-1-78243-448-1 in paperback print format
ISBN: 978-1-84317-937-5 in EPub format
ISBN: 978-1-84317-938-2 in Mobipocket format

4 5 6 7 8 9 10

Cover design by Lucy Stephens
Designed and typeset by Design 23
Maps by David Woodroffe

Printed and bound by CPI Group (UK) Ltd, Croydon, CR0 4YY

www.mombooks.com

CONTENTS

~

∽

CONFLICT AND A NEW WORLD ORDER

FOREWORD

When the original version of *I Used to Know That* was published, I spent a very jolly couple of days in a small BBC studio in central London. With headphones over my ears and a microphone in front of me, I talked to people on radio stations all over the country about the book: why I had written it, what they liked about it and what brought back hideous memories.

To my surprise, the hideous memories were what excited people most. Top of the list – and this bit *wasn't* a surprise – was maths. One listener said that just looking at the letters a + b = c on the page had brought him out in a cold sweat, even though he no longer had any idea why. Another radio station carried out a series of interviews in the street asking people, among other things, if they knew who Pythagoras was. 'Oh yes,' said one man, 'he's to do with triangles and angles and all that malarkey.'

I thought that was wonderful: 'all that malarkey' summed up perfectly the way many of my generation were taught. We had to learn it (whatever 'it' was); we were never really told why; and, once exams were over, unless we went on to be engineers or historians or something, we never thought about it again. But it lingered somewhere at the back of our minds, which may be why *I Used to Know That* touched a chord.

However, covering five major subjects and including a

catch-all chapter called General Studies meant that a single small volume couldn't hope to deal with anything in much depth. This is where the individual titles in this series come in: if *I Used to Know That* reminded us of things that we learnt once, these books will expand on them, explain why they were important and even, in the case of history, bring us up to date on things that might have been more 'current affairs' than 'history' when we were at school. If you enjoy this one, look out for *I Used to Know That: English, Geography, Maths* and *General Science* as well.

History is such a vast subject that, whether you belong to the generation that learned the dates of kings and queens or were taught in the 'daily life of a Saxon peasant' style, you can't hope to have covered everything. So *I Used to Know That: History* has two purposes: to refresh your memory of things you did once know and to fill you in on the bits that the syllabus didn't include. If your response to a mention of the Wars of the Roses is, 'Hmm, I've heard of them – what were they again?', this is the book for you. The same applies if that is your response to the Sumerians, the feudal system, the Reformation, the Indian Mutiny, the Cold War . . . the list could go on and on. From the building of the pyramids in Egypt to the fall of the Berlin Wall, everything you used to know – and much that you didn't – is here.

CAROLINE TAGGART

INTRODUCTION

When I was at school, it was fashionable to learn about history 'close up', by looking at original sources and imagining what it was like to live at the time. I have vivid memories of my history teacher becoming feverishly excited about the pre-industrial cloth-making process, bringing some yarn and a spindle into the classroom so we could all have a go. Stirring stuff, and it no doubt sparked my love of the past, but it did mean that we glossed over large areas of history, including rather important events like the Battle of Hastings (which in the good old days used to be drummed into children until they could take no more). On the other hand, many of those who learnt history in the 'old-fashioned' way – by rote and through worthy lists of dates – no doubt promptly forgot most of it as soon as they walked out of the school gates.

And yet history is arguably the most important subject taught at school – it is why we are here in the first place, after all. Just 13.5 lifespans of seventy years each will take you right back to the Norman invasion of 1066. This is one of the reasons why history is so essential to our understanding of the present; every current affairs story you read in the paper or watch on the news is somehow linked to the past. History, far from being a dusty subject, is potent and sometimes dangerous (see Nazi Germany). In the words of George Santayana, 'Those who cannot remember the past are condemned to repeat it.'

This book aims to fill in all the crucial, and rather embarrassing, gaps in your knowledge, however they got there. Key areas, stretching right back to the beginnings of civilization, are covered succinctly but comprehensively. This is emphatically *not* an academic tome: you might find the odd enlivening quotation, but you won't find great reams of primary sources (life, and this book, is simply too short). Instead, here are the essentials of the history you really should know; as well as a few extra nuggets which might surprise you (did you know, for example, that Mussolini used to be a primary school teacher?).

I hope *I Used to Know That: History* goes some way in fleshing out your hazier classroom memories and reigniting that passion for the past – and that you get as much enjoyment out of reading it as I have had researching and writing it.

EARLY CIVILIZATIONS

The first signs of civilization developed in the fertile land of Mesopotamia in around 5000 BC. Thereafter civilizations grew along the banks of the Nile, culminating in Ancient Egypt, and along the Indus River and in China. In Europe, the great city-states of Ancient Greece developed into a civilization rich in culture. Drawing heavily on its Greek forebears, Ancient Rome grew into a vast empire whose cultural legacy is still felt today. Germanic tribes eventually took over the western Roman Empire and occupied most of Europe while the eastern half flourished and became the Byzantine Empire.

PRE-CLASSICAL CIVILIZATIONS

Sumer

In about 5000 BC farmers settled on the fertile land of southern Mesopotamia (now Iraq) known as Sumer, and from these humble beginnings the world's first great civilization formed. By 3000 BC a number of city-states had developed, the largest being Ur (with a population in excess of 40,000). The Sumerians developed the first system of writing, traded in metals and wood, had skilled craftsmen, developed wheeled vehicles and had a complex administrative and legal system. Sumerian rule stretched from Syria to the Persian Gulf and lasted until about 2000 BC.

MONOTHEISM

Monotheism – the worship of one God – is thought to have emerged when the herdsman Abram, or Abraham, had a vision of the 'one true God' in the early half of the second millennium BC. The figure of Abraham is a shared spiritual forebear in Judaism, Christianity and Islam: in the Torah, Abraham is named as the ancestor of all Jews, in the Bible Jesus is descended from Abraham, the 'father of faith', and in Muslim tradition Abraham (Ibrahim) was the 'Father of the Prophets' and the ancestor of both the Jewish and Arabic peoples.

Babylon

After 2000 BC the city of Babylon (south of present-day Baghdad) grew in strength, conquering Sumer and for the first time unifying the whole of Mesopotamia. Babylon was, in all likelihood, the first city to boast a population of over 200,000. It is also known for its unashamed cult of luxury, its fortifications and the celebrated Hanging Gardens, thought to have been built by King Nebuchadnezzar II in around 605 BC. In 539 BC Babylonia was invaded and fell to the Persians.

Persia

In 550 BC Cyrus the Great conquered Assyria and became the first king of Persia. He went on to capture Babylon and by 486 BC Persia had become the biggest empire up to that point in history, covering 2 million square miles from northern India to the Mediterranean Sea, and extending through Turkey and Egypt. King Darius I introduced an effective system of administration and taxes, and the capital Persepolis (north-east of Shiraz in modern Iran) became a wealthy hub of culture and commerce. Defeat in the Persian Wars with the Greek states in the fifth century BC marked the beginning of its decline, however, and in 330 BC Persia was conquered by Alexander the Great of Macedonia.

Other early civilizations

- Minoan civilization: The Minoans founded a trading and seafaring empire, named after the legendary King Minos, centred on Crete and flourishing between 3000 and 1100 BC, making it the earliest civilization of modern Europe. They were known for their palatial architecture and development of a linear script. The Minoans were conquered by the Mycenaeans from eastern Greece in around 1450 BC.

• Indus civilization: The earliest recorded complex urban civilization on the Indian Subcontinent developed along the valley of the River Indus in modern Pakistan from about 2500 BC to 1500 BC. The Indus people developed urban planning, with straight streets and drains, as well as decorative stonework, irrigation and a complex script.

• Hittite Empire: Stretching from the east of modern Ankara to the Mediterranean coast and northern Syria, the Hittite Empire flourished from around 1700 to *c.*1200 BC, when it disintegrated under attack from Assyria.

• Shang dynasties: Chinese tradition has it that the Xia dynasty ruled in the Yellow River Valley before the first recorded dynasty of the Shang took over around 1600 BC. They followed a complex calendar, developed intricate jade carving and made musical instruments. The Shang dynasty was taken over by the Zhou warriors in around 1046 BC. In this period there were developments in agriculture, silk weaving and the study of philosophy (most notably by Confucius).

- Olmec civilization: Centred on the Gulf of Mexico this was thought to be the first civilization in Meso-America, coming to prominence, around 1500 BC. They were skilled stonemasons and created huge carved heads and monuments.

- Assyrian Empire: The Assyrian state established itself around 1300 BC, and its empire reached its greatest extent in the seventh century BC, after which it was absorbed by the Persians.

ANCIENT EGYPT

Ancient Egypt formed from the settlements that had grown along the banks of the Nile in north-eastern Africa from around 5000 BC. In about 3200 BC records tell us that the kingdoms of Egypt were unified in a single state 600 miles long. This was the beginning of a civilization that was to survive for 3,000 years, into the age of Ancient Greece and Rome. Egypt's cultural and technological achievements were many, not least the construction of its monumental pyramids (tombs for their ruling families) and temples.

The history of Egypt is generally divided into the relatively stable periods of the Old, Middle and New Kingdoms, separated by periods of instability. The period known as the Old Kingdom (*c.*2664–2155 BC) was ruled over by powerful pharaohs and saw major developments in technology, art and architecture. Hieroglyphic script was developed and papyrus paper invented. The first stepped pyramid was built at Saqqara as well as the vast pyramids at Giza (the only surviving Wonders of the World).

After a period of famine and strife, stability was once more restored when Mentuhotep II reunited Egypt. It was during this era, the Middle Kingdom (*c.*2052–1786 BC), that the worship of Osiris, god of death and rebirth, spread across Egypt, offering the hope of afterlife to all Egyptians, not just the pharaoh. However, the power of the pharaohs ultimately weakened, with the north and south being taken over by other dynasties.

The pharaohs re-established control during the final Egyptian age of the New Kingdom (*c.*1554–1075 BC), extending their influence into Syria, Nubia and the Middle East. This is regarded as the greatest chapter of Egypt's history, during which many temples were built, including the painted tombs in the Valley of the Kings. During this era Hatshepsut, the first female pharaoh, came to power, as well as the boy-king Tutankhamen and Rameses II, who ruled for a remarkable sixty-seven years.

After these three great ages, Egypt went into slow decline, though the influence of Egyptian culture was to be felt for hundreds of years. Over the following centuries they faced successive invasions by the Libyans, Assyrians and

Persians. Egypt gained independence briefly in the early part of the fourth century, then in 332 BC Alexander the Great occupied Egypt and his general Ptolemy became pharaoh. New temples in the Egyptian style were built and Alexandria was established as the capital and a seat of learning.

Cleopatra VII, history's famous femme fatale, ruled in the years leading up to Rome's conquest of Egypt in 30 BC.

ANCIENT GREECE

Following the fall of the Mycenaean civilization in the Aegean in the twelfth century BC, the Greeks rose in power. Ancient Greece began as a loose association of city-states that were frequently at war, and evolved into one of the greatest empires ever seen. The Ancient Greeks made advances in philosophy, science, mathematics, art, trade, architecture and literature, all of which profoundly influenced the Roman Empire, as well as all subsequent civilizations in the West.

The history of Ancient Greece is often divided into four distinct periods: Archaic, Classical, Hellenistic and Roman. It was during the Archaic Period (c.750–490 BC) that Athens, Sparta, Corinth and Thebes emerged as the dominant city-states. The first Olympian Games were held, Homer composed the epic poems the *Iliad* and the

THE BIRTH OF DEMOCRACY

In the fifth century, Athens successfully repulsed a
Spartan invasion; then, in a bid to avoid tyrannical
rule by local rich landowners, the people of Athens
established the world's first democracy (from the
Greek *demokratia* 'rule of the people'). All citizens
had equal privileges, although non-citizens – slaves,
females or foreigners – had no rights at all.

Odyssey, Pythagoras developed his theory and the Greeks
established trading posts as far away as the Nile Delta.
Syracuse in Sicily and Byzantium on the Bosporus became
major trading centres and Greece as a whole prospered.

Classical Greece (*c.*490–336 BC) is known as the greatest
age of Greek history. The Greeks were united when they
defeated the Persians, and the Parthenon was built in
Athens in celebration. It was in this period that democracy
became fully established under Pericles, the great tragedies
of Euripides were written and the philosophies of Plato
and Sophocles developed.

The conquest of Greece in 338 BC by Philip II of
Macedonia's and the subsequent rule of Alexander III,

better known as Alexander the Great, mark the beginning of the Hellenistic Period (*c.*336–146 BC). During this time, the philosopher Aristotle (who also tutored Alexander the Great) composed much of his work. Greek culture and language were exported to the newly acquired Hellenistic kingdoms around the Mediterranean and Asia Minor. Alexandria in Egypt and Antioch in Syria became the new centres of Hellenistic culture, while the city-states of Greece declined in influence.

After the death of Alexander, the city-states secured some freedom for themselves, but it all came to an end in 146 BC, when Greece was finally incorporated into the greatest empire yet, Rome. The Greek peninsula became an eastern province of the Roman Empire. Nonetheless, Greek ideas and culture permeated much of Roman society, and the Greek language thrived as the lingua franca of the eastern part of the Roman Empire.

THE ROMAN EMPIRE

The civilization of Ancient Rome was to last for more than a thousand years, eventually encompassing most of western and northern Europe, North Africa and the Middle East. As the Roman Empire spread over the globe, so did its language, art, technological innovations and administrative systems; Roman influences are still shared today by countries thousands of miles apart. In the end, a victim of its own success, the empire became hopelessly unwieldy and overstretched, making it vulnerable to attack from the fierce tribes of northern Europe.

Early Rome

Fact and legend rub shoulders together in the accounts of the origins of Rome. The legend picturesquely suggests that Rome was founded in 735 BC by the twin brothers Romulus and Remus, the abandoned sons of the war-god Mars. However, historical sources are less romantic; Rome began as a cluster of settlements on the seven hills beside the River Tiber, which by 600 BC had joined together to form a city. Rome was initially ruled by the Etruscans, rich traders from central Italy.

The Republic

In 509 BC Roman nobles drove out the seventh Etruscan king of Rome, Tarquin the Proud, and Rome became a republic, ruled by two consuls elected from the senate. The Roman state was called the *Res Publica*, 'public thing' (from which we take the word 'republic'). Rome grew in strength, gradually overpowering the other peoples on the Italian peninsula, including the Etruscans and Greek settlers.

In the mid third century BC Rome clashed with Carthage in North Africa, leading to the Punic Wars (264–146 BC). It was during these wars that the

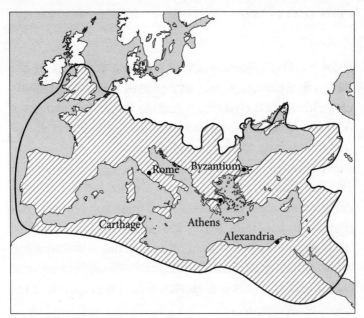

The Greatest Extent of the Roman Empire

Carthaginian general Hannibal famously marched his war elephants over the Alps, smashing the Roman legions at the Battle of Cannae in 216 BC. By 146 BC Rome had secured her first overseas possessions – Sicily, Spain and North Africa – and the subsequent Macedonian Wars left Rome dominant in Macedonia, Greece and parts of Asia Minor.

Julius Caesar conquered Gaul (now France) in 51 BC and, after a period of civil war, appointed himself dictator for life. The senators responded by having him assassinated, leading to disorder and a struggle for dominance until Julius Caesar's adopted son Octavian defeated Mark Antony and Cleopatra of Egypt at the Battle of Actium in 31 BC (when Egypt was also annexed). Octavian took the name Augustus, 'the revered one', and became the first emperor of Rome in 27 BC. Imperial rule was to continue for the next 400 years.

The Pax Romana

Augustus's reign spanned forty-one years and brought with it peace and stability. While thousands of troops guarded the frontiers of the Roman Empire, Augustus continued to improve its infrastructure, with the building of roads and great buildings. When Augustus died, the senate declared him a Roman god.

The period from the rule of Augustus and the death of Marcus Aurelius in AD 180 is often called the Pax Romana (Roman peace), when the empire was relatively free from internal or external threat. Emperors from this period varied in capability and, indeed, popularity; the most notorious being Caligula, who was perhaps unfairly portrayed by the Roman historian Tacitus as insane and a sexual pervert, and Nero, a cruel tyrant who ordered the burning of Christians. Other emperors fared rather better: Claudius conquered Britain (see page 27); Trajan expanded the empire to its greatest extent; and Hadrian ensured the provinces were well-governed, built his eponymous wall in the north of England and sensibly limited any further expansion.

ROMAN INNOVATIONS

Architecture: Roman architecture drew heavily from Greek styles, but their great use of arches and the invention of the dome became their hallmark styles. The invention of concrete allowed Romans to build more ambitious and durable structures, like the Colosseum.

Heating: The Romans also developed underfloor heating – the hypocaust system – often used for bathhouses or wealthy villas. The floor of a room would be raised on pillars so that hot air from a furnace could circulate in the hollow space and heat the room above.

Plumbing: The Romans designed numerous aqueducts to feed the public water fountains where most people fetched their daily supplies. Large private houses, bathhouses and public toilets eventually had indoor plumbing, using a network of lead pipes.

Roads: The Roman road system spanned over 250,000 miles. They developed a form of concrete to produce a waterproof hard surface. Many of their typically straight routes form the basis of the roads in use today.

The Crisis of the Third Century

A series of incompetent and lesser-known emperors ruled after the Pax Romana, leading to a long period of imperial collapse, dramatically known as the Crisis of the Third Century. European and Asian enemies challenged Rome's power on many occasions, notably in AD 260 when Emperor Valerian was defeated by the Persians at the Battle of Edessa in Turkey.

The empire groaned under the weight of an unwieldy administrative system and an increasingly powerless army. In AD 286, Emperor Diocletian decided to split the empire into eastern and western halves. Diocletian took charge of the eastern half and set up his government in Turkey, and Maximian, the general in command of Gaul, took control of the western half.

In AD 324 Emperor Constantine I retook command of the whole Roman Empire and established the Greek town of Byzantium as the capital, renaming it Constantinople, thereby establishing the Byzantine Empire (see page 29). When Constantine's successor Theodosius I died in AD 395, the empire was again divided into east and west.

The Decline of the Roman Empire

As the Byzantine Empire thrived in the east, the Western Roman Empire was increasingly weakened by battles with Germanic tribes and the so-called Barbarian people to the north. In AD 406 the Rhine frontier was overrun and Germanic tribes poured into the empire (see page 30), finally sacking Rome itself in AD 455. In AD 476 the last Roman emperor, Romulus Augustus, was forced to abdicate and the Western Roman Empire finally collapsed.

Roman Britain

In AD 43 Emperor Claudius used infighting between British tribes to his advantage and invaded Britain. Within a few years southern Britain was duly Romanized; Roman laws, roads and towns were established and for 400 years Britain was part of the Roman Empire (though the rule of Rome never extended beyond Hadrian's Wall, to western Wales or indeed across the sea to Ireland). Camulodunum (now Colchester) was made the first capital of the new Roman province of Britannia, although this soon switched to Londinium (London), its situation on the Thames more convenient for trade.

To house their great legions, the Romans built forts all around the country and British towns grew up around them. The Romans also constructed roads, amphitheatres, temples, bridges and bathhouses and introduced sophisticated water and sewage systems. However, the Celtic influence and way of life continued alongside and, while Latin was the official language of government, army and trade, the majority of Britons still spoke in Celtic languages.

CELTIC REBELLION

During their occupation of Britain, the Romans often met fierce opposition from Celtic tribes: an *eighth* of the entire Roman army was needed to garrison Britain. Around AD 60 the Romans faced an uprising so serious that they nearly lost Britain completely. Boudicca was the thorn in their side: she and her rebellious tribes laid waste to Colchester, Londinium and Verulamium (St Albans). They outnumbered the Roman forces by about twenty to one, but the superior discipline and military efficiency of the Roman army led them to victory, with a reported loss of life of 80,000 Britons.

The Emperor Hadrian ordered the building of a defensive frontier wall between Roman Britain and Scotland in AD 122 to protect against the warlike Picts. However increasing attacks from the Picts, and the invading Germanic tribes of the Angles, Saxons and Jutes, along with Barbaric invasion across the empire, led to the Romans eventually pulling out of Britain at the beginning of the fifth century.

The Byzantine Empire

The Byzantine Empire was established in AD 330 when the Roman Emperor Constantine I moved his capital from Rome to the Greek town of Byzantine in the eastern empire. Renaming it Constantinople (now Istanbul), a new city was built where Greek and Roman culture was preserved and treasures from all over the empire adorned its new buildings.

Constantine was the first Christian emperor; he reversed the anti-Christian laws of Emperor Diocletian, promoted religious tolerance and made Christianity the official religion of Constantinople. While Barbaric invaders ravaged the Western Empire, eventually leading to its collapse in AD 476 (see page 31), the Byzantine Empire continued to thrive, protected by huge walls and fortifications.

Constantinople became the hub of a major trading network that extended across Europe, Asia and North Africa, and the city itself became famous for its wealth, art and architecture. From AD 527, Christian Emperor Justinian I further expanded the empire by conquering North Africa and parts of Italy, so that by his death in AD 565 the Byzantine Empire stretched from Spain to Persia. Constantinople was finally captured by the Ottoman Turks in 1453, marking the final collapse of the Byzantine Empire.

THE BEGINNINGS OF EUROPE

As the Roman Empire weakened, a great movement of Germanic tribes overran Europe in search of land and new settlements (sometimes known as the 'Great Migration'). Europe gradually became more Germanic in nature, as hoards of tribespeople poured into the Western Roman Empire, eventually leading to its collapse. Out of this turmoil emerged new kingdoms, including the Frankish nation, whose powerful leaders successfully fought off Arab invasion and extended the influence of Christianity in Europe. Old-fashioned history books perhaps unfairly referred to this period as the 'Dark Ages' (a term first coined by the Renaissance writer Petrarch) as much of the language and culture of classical antiquity disappeared and few records of the period survive.

THE GOTHS AND THE VANDALS

During the third and fourth centuries, the Germanic tribes of the heterogeneous Goths and Vandals migrated from the Baltic region to settle in the Lower Danube and Black Sea area of Europe. Driven south by migrating Huns in AD 376, the Visigoths (Goths from the west) defeated and killed

Roman Emperor Valens at Adrianople in AD 378. A decisive moment in the eventual fall of Rome, it forced the Romans to negotiate with the Visigoths and accommodate them within the empire. Under the leadership of King Alaric, the Visigoths eventually laid siege to Rome itself in AD 410. In order to defend their great capital, the Romans were forced to recall their troops from frontier garrisons in Gaul and Britain and on the Rhine and Danube, thus allowing other Germanic tribes to burst through the empire's borders. The Vandals eventually sailed to North Africa when they set up an independent kingdom in Carthage in AD 439, only to return to Italy, ravage Sicily and eventually sack Rome in AD 455. The last Roman emperor, Romulus Augustulus, was overthrown in AD 476. The Vandals and Ostrogoths (Goths from the east) were eventually crushed by Byzantine generals in the sixth century, and the Visigoths who had settled in Spain were ultimately defeated by the Franks in AD 507 and absorbed by Muslim invaders by AD 720.

THE HUNS

The Huns, a formidable nomadic race originating from central Asia, swept into Europe at the end of the fourth century. There they defeated the Ostrogoths, then the Visigoths and other barbarian people as they advanced west. Their great leader Attila (r. AD 434–53), whom

ISLAMIC CALIPHATES

In around AD 610 an Arab merchant, Muhammad, had a vision in which he was instructed to preach a new faith centred on one true God, Allah. As he delivered his message, he attracted many supporters and the new faith of Islam (meaning 'submitting to the will of God') spread throughout Arabia. Between the seventh and eighth centuries Islamic rule expanded rapidly under the Umayad caliphs (ruling dynasties) to become one of the largest empires in history. The Arabic Islamic Empire encroached upon the Christian Byzantine Empire and eventually stretched from the borders of China to North Africa and into the Iberian Peninsula (from where they invaded France – see page 34).

With the ascension of the Abbasid caliphate in AD 750, the capital shifted from Harran to Baghdad and the Golden Age of Islam followed. Lasting until around the thirteenth century, this period witnessed a revitalization of scholarly and religious thought and resulted in major developments in the realms of agriculture, the arts, sciences, law, medicine, mathematics, industry, economics and literature.

contemporary Christian writers described as 'the scourge of God', further expanded and unified their empire. However in AD 451 the Huns suffered successive defeat at the hands of the Romans, Visigoths and Franks, and following Attila's death two years later, the Hunnic Empire began to disintegrate. Their subsequent movement westward displaced other barbarian people in Europe, contributing to the 'Great Migration' and the collapse of the Roman Empire. After the Hunnic Empire collapsed around the fifth century, the Slavs of eastern Europe (known as the Scythians and Sarmatians by the Romans) migrated Westwards into the void it left behind, towards the Baltic, the Adriatic and the Black Sea.

THE LOMBARDS

The Lombards were a Germanic tribe who migrated from the north to settle on the Hungarian Plains, east of the River Elbe. With pressure from other invading tribes from the west, in AD 568 they invaded and occupied Italy. The northern areas were conquered by Charlemagne in AD 774 and absorbed into the Frankish Empire but the Lombard kingdoms of southern Italy remained independent until the mid eleventh century, before being overcome by the Normans.

THE FRANKS AND THE HOLY ROMAN EMPIRE

The Franks were a group of Germanic tribes who, under the Merovingian dynasty, eventually settled in Gaul. The Frankish state of Gaul (which eventually became known as Francia) gradually consolidated its hold on neighbouring kingdoms so that by the end of the eighth century the Franks dominated much of western Europe. In AD 732, the Frankish king Charles Martel fought off the invasion of Arab forces at Poitiers, thereby preventing Arab domination in France and western Europe. Martel's grandson, Charlemagne (see opposite) later ruled over the Frankish Empire (also called the Carolingian Empire) which covered France, part of Spain and Germany and much of Italy. Made up of a union of central European territories, the Holy Roman Empire was a key driving force behind the Crusades (see page 47) and lasted for over a thousand years, with Napoleon abolishing it in 1806.

The Expansion of Christianity
In western Europe, Christian missionaries began to convert Germanic settlers, who had originally worshipped their own pagan gods. In around AD 500 the Italian St Benedict set out his Monastic Rule and monasteries began to be established in Europe, often as great centres of learning, most notably on the outposts of Ireland and the British Isles. Ireland was largely

CHARLEMAGNE (C.742–814)

Crowned king of the Franks in AD 768, Charlemagne (meaning 'Charles the Great') was an energetic and powerful leader, who in AD 772 instigated a thirty-year campaign to conquer and Christianize Europe. Having supported Popes Hadrian I and , later, Leo III in ridding Italy of the Lombards, he was invited to Rome and crowned Holy Roman Emperor on Christmas Day AD 800. Charlemagne also worked hard to improve the standard of living for his own people in Aachen by promoting new farming techniques and setting up a monetary system to advance commerce. He was also a major proponent of education and under his rule the Carolingian Renaissance revived the arts and scholarly thinking.

Christian by the early sixth century mainly due to the missionary zeal of St Patrick in the previous century. Thereafter, Irish monks began to make their way to Britain, Gaul and Germany, founding monasteries and frequently acting as advisers to the Christian kings of the Frankish kingdom. In the late sixth century Pope Gregory the Great sent out missions to spread Christianity in Britain. St Augustine led one of these missions and converted King Ethelbert of Kent, becoming the first Archbishop of Canterbury (not to be confused with St Augustine of Hippo, the philosopher who would later influence Protestantism). St Columba meanwhile had arrived in Scotland from Ireland and converted the northern Picts, and St David had established monasteries in Wales and the west of England. By the late seventh century, Christianity had spread across Britain.

The East–West Schism

In the eighth and ninth centuries, increasing theological and political differences between Constantinople and Rome led to permanent division of the Christian Church in Europe, known as the East-West Schism. In 1054, Constantinople broke with the Church in Rome to form the Eastern Orthodox Church.

THE ANGLES, SAXONS AND JUTES

The Angles, Saxons and Jutes were Germanic-speaking peoples who invaded and settled in Britain between the fifth and seventh centuries. Their migration from

Germany and the Jutland peninsula in modern-day Denmark formed part of the general movement of Germanic people throughout Europe at this time. By AD 600 the south and east of England were established as Anglo-Saxon kingdoms.

Anglo-Saxon Settlements in Britain

The early Anglo-Saxons settlers were a farming people, for whom the manor houses were the centres of their settlements. Land was divided into 'hides', each hide enough to support one peasant farmer or 'churl' and his family. Anyone who owned more than five hides of land was known as a 'thane', and the most loyal of these lived with the king and were expected to witness the king's public actions and, if necessary, fight and die for him.

The west and north of Britain remained under the control of Celtic-speaking Britons. In the north the Picts, who had resisted the Romans, controlled a portion of Scotland, while the Celtic-speaking Scots, who had come over from Ireland, controlled the kingdom of Dalriada on the west coast.

By the eighth century, the Anglo-Saxon English, while not fully united, were becoming more aware of themselves as an ethnic and cultural identity. Trade was on the increase and coins were more widely used. Letters survive from Saxon kings and scholars, and poets began composing poems with a feel of their ethnicity –

the most famous being the epic *Beowulf*. In AD 731 the Northumbrian monk Bede completed his work *The Ecclesiastical History of the English People*, which is one of our main (though not always accurate) written sources for the Anglo-Saxon period.

THE VIKINGS

'In this year Beorhtric [King of Wessex] took to wife Eadburh, daughter of King Offa. And in his days came first three ships of Norwegians from Hörthaland: and then the reeve rode thither and tried to compel them to go to the royal manor, for he did not know what they were: and then they slew him. These were the first ships of the Danes to come to England.'

This ominous entry under the year AD 789 in *The Anglo-Saxon Chronicle* (written by scribes in Britain around the ninth century) describes the first of many bloody Viking raids in Britain. Over the next sixty years, Vikings from areas now known as Denmark, Sweden and Norway arrived in ships and looted from the local inhabitants. Often targeting churches and monasteries, their attacks were sudden and ferocious.

The Vikings seized Scottish and Irish coastal areas and most of northern and eastern England. The invasions of

SCOTTISH AND WELSH RESISTANCE TO THE VIKINGS

In around AD 841 the king of Dalriada, Kenneth MacAlpine, drove the Vikings out of his own kingdom, then invaded the Pictish kingdoms of Scotland, uniting them under one rule and becoming king of the Picts in AD 843.

In the west, Rhodri Mawr (or Rhodri the Great), prince of Gwynedd, also fought off Viking invaders, as well as English armies, and came to rule most of Wales. While his kingdom collapsed after his death, the principle of a dynasty of Welsh rulers lived on.

Britain formed part of a major raiding campaign by the Vikings, who between the eighth and eleventh centuries attacked the coastlines of Europe, rowing inland along the Loire, Rhine and other rivers. They travelled as far as Russia from the Baltic and threatened Constantinople, sailing vast distances to 'raid and trade', and making the first known voyages to Iceland, Greenland and North America.

The Vikings were expert shipbuilders, with sturdy ships to carry cargo (*knorrs*) and faster longships for raiding and fishing (*langskips*). These boats had such shallow hulls that they could row up a river or land on a beach without a quay. Despite their image as marauding barbarians, the Vikings brought to the areas they invaded not only shipbuilding knowledge but also trade, fine decorative metalwork and the poetry of their epic sagas.

Alfred the Great

In the ninth century, the most powerful kingdom in England was Wessex. Alfred, King of Wessex, spent the first few years of his reign fighting the Vikings, and was pushed back to Athelney, Somerset. However, in AD 878 he finally routed the main Viking army at the Battle of Ethandune and captured London in 886. He then negotiated the division of England into two halves – the Vikings were to keep the north and east under Danish rule, the Danelaw, and the rest of England would remain under Saxon control.

The only English king to be called 'the Great', Alfred encouraged a revival in learning, reformed Saxon law, established an efficient administration and commissioned a history of the English people, *The Anglo-Saxon Chronicle*. He reorganized and fortified his army and navy, and built a number of fortified towns. Alfred assumed the title 'King of the Anglo-Saxons' and it was under his rule that his subjects began to call themselves *Angelcynn* – the English.

THE BURNING OF THE CAKES

Despite a string of great achievements, Alfred is remembered for a well-known, though apocryphal, story involving baking. It is said that during his campaign against the Vikings in Somerset, he took refuge with a peasant woman who, unaware of his identity, asked him to watch over some cakes she had left on the fire. Distracted by plans of battle, he let them burn, only to be ticked off by the woman. She swiftly apologized once she realized who he was, but Alfred insisted that it was he who should apologize.

THE NORMANS

The Normans were descendants of earlier Vikings (their name is derived from 'Norsemen'), as well as the Franks and Romans, who had settled in northern France. They were sympathetic to the plight of their Danish cousins and frequently gave shelter to the Vikings after their raids on Britain and other areas of western Europe. In order to prevent this, the English King Ethelred II (nicknamed Ethelred the Unready) made a treaty with the Duke of

Normandy, in which each promised not to aid the other's enemies. Ten years later he consolidated the pact by marrying the Duke's sister, Emma, in 1002. Thus began the association of Normandy with England.

By the time of Ethelred's death in 1016, there was dissent and confusion and the Viking King Canute seized the throne. Following the reigns of Canute's sons Harold Harefoot and Hardecanute, the throne returned to Saxon rule under Edward the Confessor in 1043. Edward returned from exile in Normandy where he had befriended many Norman nobles, including William, Duke of Normandy, the future Conqueror.

The Battle of Hastings

When Edward died in 1066 without an heir, several contenders, including William of Normandy, stepped forward to claim the throne. William and the powerful English lord Harold Godwinson both claimed that Edward had named *him* as the heir. The king's council of chief advisers – the Witan – needed to settle the matter quickly and immediately crowned Harold king of England.

Shortly afterwards, *another* contender for the throne, Harald Hardrada of Norway, invaded Northumbria and occupied York. In September 1066, King Harold met and defeated the Norwegian forces at the Battle of Stamford Bridge near York and recovered Northumbria. In the meantime, William's fleet landed on the south coast. Harold's

THE DOMESDAY BOOK

In 1086 William I commissioned an immense survey to find out the value of his newly conquered country and maximize its tax revenues. It was a comprehensive assessment of property and land and one of the grandest administrative achievements of the era. Scribes were dispatched across the length and breadth of the country to ask landowners detailed questions about their property, who they lived with, and even the number of ploughs they owned. The survey was only later nicknamed the Domesday Book, in reference to God's last day of judgement. These days, thanks to the National Archives website, it is available for all to view online.

exhausted army rushed southwards to confront a Norman force three times its size.

The armies met on 14 October on a hill near Hastings. Though the English forces put up a strong defence, the Normans had the advantage of strength and numbers and the English were overcome. Harold died on the battlefield – the scene gruesomely depicted in the Bayeux Tapestry, an arrow piercing his eye. William the Conqueror was crowned William I, King of England at Westminster Abbey on Christmas Day 1066. The Normans also went on to conquer Wales, some of Ireland, parts of Scotland, southern Italy and Sicily.

From this point on, the Normans and their descendants replaced the Anglo-Saxons as the ruling class of England. Closely aligned with France, the early Norman kings and nobility held land on both sides of the channel and were predominantly French-speaking. Eventually, however, the distinction between Norman and English blurred so that by the 1300s the Norman aristocracy thought of themselves as English.

THE MIDDLE AGES

Europe in the Middle Ages witnessed a terrible pandemic, huge social change, rebellion and a conflict between religions that rumbles on to this day. The Black Death wiped out nearly a third of the population of Europe, and in the process sowed the seeds for future social change. The Middle East also became a battleground between Christian and Muslim Empires, as new ideas and goods were exchanged along with bloody blows.

MEDIEVAL LIFE

The political and economic system of feudalism is thought to have emerged as a stabilizing influence in Europe after the collapse of the Roman Empire. Feudal relationships could be complex and sometimes ambiguous, but contractual obligations based around the tenure of land and the provision of military service were the building blocks of medieval society in Europe.

In Norman England, as in much of the rest of Europe, kings leased lands known as 'fiefs' to powerful lords or vassals in return for their allegiance and homage. The lords then divided their lands into manors or estates, which they leased to lesser nobles or knights. Similarly, religious institutions might own estates for which tenants or lesser nobles were obliged to pay homage. At the very bottom of the social heap was a class of unfree peasants (villeins or serfs) who lived – and died – under the jurisdiction of the lord.

A MEDIEVAL MANOR

At the head of a typical estate or manor stood a nobleman with land set aside for himself (usually the bigger part) and the rest divided into smallholdings to lease to his tenants, who were obliged to work the nobleman's land in addition to their own. A holding was a share (usually a strip) of a large, unfenced field. Each field would contain a different crop to form part of a simple rotation and in addition there would be common land where tenants could graze livestock.

The estate was a self-sufficient unit where everything produced was for consumption and not for sale. After a bad harvest, or in times of scarcity, locals might depend heavily on their lord's provisions if they were to avoid starvation.

The Crusades

In 1095 Pope Urban II, in response to a plea for help from the Christian Byzantines, who were under attack from Muslim Turks (see page 48), called upon the nobility of western Europe to come to their defence in the First Crusade. This was the beginning of almost two centuries of military campaigns in the Middle East. The aim of the Crusades was to recapture the Christian Holy Lands of Syria and Palestine from their Islamic rulers. The Crusades were frequently marked by their brutality and increasingly fought as much for commercial gain as spiritual salvation. Despite almost two hundred years of sporadic conflict, most of Palestine remained in Muslim hands.

The First Crusade included armies from France, Germany and southern Italy as well as many volunteers and was led by Godfrey de Bouillon. It succeeded in recapturing Jerusalem in 1099; the city's Muslim inhabitants were massacred and a new kingdom established. Fifty years on, the Second Crusade, called by Pope Eugene III, was led by Louis VII of France and Conrad III of Germany and was a failure.

The Third Crusade (or Kings' Crusade) was instigated by the peaceful capture of Jerusalem in 1187 by Saladin, Sultan of Egypt and Syria. Led by Philip II of France and Richard I of England, better known as Richard the Lionheart, the Crusaders succeeded in recapturing the

THE REACH OF ISLAM

In the mid eleventh century, a wandering group of Muslim Turks (the Seljuks) took over the Abbasid lands (see page 32), captured Byzantium in 1071, established their own ruling dynasty and then settled in large numbers across Asia Minor (thereby precipitating the Crusades). The Turkish language and Islam replaced Christianity in much of the region.

By the early part of the thirteenth century, Mongols (nomads from central Asia whose greatest leader took the name of Genghis Khan) overran Muslim lands following their conquest of China, their empire stretching from the Black Sea to the Pacific. In the following century, Mongol power declined and new principalities were created in Byzantium. This included one created by Osman I, which gradually expanded into the Ottoman Empire. Capturing Constantinople in 1453, the Ottoman Empire reached its zenith under Sultan Suleiman the Magnificent in the sixteenth century when the Ottomans dominated south-eastern Europe, the Middle East and North Africa.

city of Acre, but failed to take Jerusalem. Richard made a truce with Saladin and returned home in 1192.

At the beginning of the thirteenth century, the Fourth Crusade was authorized by Pope Innocent III. Diverted by Venetian commercial interests, instead of freeing the Holy Land, it sacked Constantinople instead. The Fifth Crusade (1218) captured and then lost the Egyptian port of Damietta. Jerusalem was recovered during the Sixth Crusade by means of negotiation with the Sultan of Egypt . . . but lost again in 1244.

The Seventh and Eighth Crusades in the mid to late thirteenth century were both led by Louis IX of France, who was taken prisoner for a hefty ransom during the Seventh, and contracted an illness and died during the Eighth. (Louis IX was later declared a saint by Pope Boniface VIII – the only French king ever to have been canonized.) Acre, the last Christian fortress, fell in 1291, marking the end of the Crusaders' ambitions.

The Knights Templar and Malta

The Knights Templar was an international religious military order founded in about 1120 by a band of knights who vowed to protect Christian pilgrims travelling to the Holy Land. In battle they wore characteristic white robes with red crosses. Another Christian military order was the Knights Hospitallers, who in 1070 ran a hospital for sick pilgrims in Jerusalem, with Muslim permission. From

MEDIEVAL CHIVALRY

A distinctive code of conduct emerged from the
privileged position of being a mounted knight or
'chevalier' (from which we get the word chivalry).
Knights were expected to be honourable, courageous,
loyal to the king, courteous, especially towards women,
and generous. Many Crusaders did not uphold this
ideal, but there were some, most famously Richard I
(the Lionheart), who were heralded for their chivalrous
deeds. Saladin, Sultan of Egypt, was famed for his
knightly qualities and held up as an ideal in western
societies. Richard and Saladin, though enemies, were
said to have held each other in high regard, each
recognizing a worthy opponent in the other.

1530 they were known as the Knights of Malta, having been
given the island by Holy Roman Emperor Charles V. Malta
was strategically important for trade as well as pilgrimage
(and for that reason would be later occupied by the French
and the British, before being granted independence in
1964). Both orders attracted noble members, and grew
immensely wealthy and powerful.

Commercial Gains of the Crusades

Trade flourished throughout the Middle East and Europe during the Crusades and the Crusaders were accompanied by a retinue of clerics, scholars and merchants – all of whom had their own interests. Exotic Middle Eastern goods were introduced to Europe, such as lemons, dates, sugar, coffee, diamonds, cotton, gunpowder, writing paper, mirrors and carpets. New scientific ideas and inventions, such as Arabic numerical figures, algebra, water wheels and clocks, chemistry and irrigation, were also introduced.

The Crusaders were not averse to the odd spot of plundering and the British Museum, the Louvre and other European institutes still house treasures and relics brought back from the Crusades.

MAGNA CARTA

Richard I, the Crusader king, was succeeded by his brother John, an unpopular ruler who lost vast territories in France and continually squeezed his unhappy subjects with higher and higher taxes to pay for his military humiliations overseas. In 1215 his barons had had enough and they forced him to agree to their terms at Runnymede. The barons duly drew up Magna Carta (the Great Charter), a document limiting the king's powers, and the first of its kind to be forced on an English monarch. Though King John gave the document his Great Seal, he did not stick to his word and the First Barons' War soon erupted, a conflict that was to continue into the reign of John's son, Henry III.

Magna Carta is arguably Britain's most famous legal document. However, in spite of its fame, only three of its sixty-three clauses are still recognized by English law. One of these, quoted below, guarantees the rights of individual subjects, leading some to claim that Magna Carta was a proclamation of the rights of common men, though in reality it was drawn up to protect the interests of the wealthy few. Many copies of the original charter were made and dispatched across the land, but only four remain in existence today: one in Lincoln Castle, one in Salisbury Cathedral and two in the British Library.

> 'No free man shall be arrested or imprisoned . . . or outlawed or exiled or victimized in any other way . . . except by the lawful judgement of his peers or by the law of the land.'
>
> (MAGNA CARTA, ARTICLE 39)

THE BLACK DEATH

The Black Death swept through Europe and the Middle East in the mid fourteenth century and was the most virulent and terrifying form of bubonic and pneumonic plague ever recorded. It is thought to have killed about a third of the total European population – about 25 million people – by the time it died out in 1351.

The origins of the plague are uncertain, but it is believed to have started in the 1330s in the Far East by germ-bearing fleas carried on rodents. From China (where it is said to have killed 13 million people), it rapidly spread westwards along the Silk Road. It then hit the Byzantine Empire with devastating ferocity (in Constantinople, they called it the 'Great Dying'). By 1348 it had reached cities in France, Spain and England, and a year later it had spread to Germany, Russia, Scandinavia and then parts of the Middle East.

The first signs of the Black Death were a high fever and black swellings or hard pus-filled boils, appearing first on the armpits, groin and neck, and then all over the body. Most people who were infected died within forty-eight hours. The clothes of the dead were then burned and bodies were taken away by cart and buried in a deep pit. There was no cure and no preventative treatment. To put it bluntly: you were done for.

Nevertheless, in desperation people turned to various

THE SILK ROAD

The Silk Road (silk being one of China's main exports) was an ancient caravan route that linked China with the West. Following the conquests of Mongol leader Genghis Khan, by the 1300s the entire length of the Silk Road was under the control of a vast Mongolian Empire extending from south-eastern Asia to eastern Europe. This facilitated the free passage of Mongolian armies, traders and other travellers who inadvertently hastened the spread of the Black Death.

unsuccessful 'cures' and treatments, which included lancing the pus-filled boils, bleeding the patient, witchcraft (one spell involved placing a live hen next to the swelling in order to draw out the disease) and foul-smelling lotions made from eggs, flour, honey and turpentine. None of these were successful and most were likely to speed up the demise of the unhappy patient.

The Hundred Years Wars

England had controlled a large amount of land in France since the reign of William I, and there was continual friction between the two nations over territories. After Philip IV of France confiscated Aquitaine in 1337, Edward III of England responded by claiming the French crown, thus setting off a series of wars that would last 116 years and bankrupt the English crown. At the outset the English were victorious and Edward defeated Philip at Crécy in 1346, aided by his son, also Edward, dubbed the Black Prince for the colour of his armour.

THE LONGBOW

The English victory at the Battle of Crécy has been credited largely to the use of the English longbow, which could shoot arrows faster and be reloaded more quickly than the heavy crossbows used by the French. It revolutionized land warfare and was used to devastating effect at Crécy where the French are thought to have lost over 10,000 men, the English 200.

The wind of fortune soon blew the other way and in 1360 Edward, after several defeats, gave up his claim to the French throne in return for the substantially enlarged territory of Aquitaine. However, land was gradually lost to the French under the leadership of a new king, Charles V, and by the time of Edward's death in 1377, only Calais, Bordeaux and Bayonne remained under English rule.

In the fifteenth century, war was declared once more by Henry V (captured so memorably in Shakespeare's eponymous play), who renewed the English claim to the French throne. In 1415 he invaded France and famously defeated the French at the Battle of Agincourt; the English once more outnumbered by the French (perhaps by as much as two to one).

After Henry's sudden death on campaign, possibly of dysentery, his brother John, Duke of Bedford, acted as regent in France for Henry's young son Henry VI. Bedford had several successes until Joan of Arc, the 'Maid of Orléans', led the French to victory in 1429. Over the next few years England lost the majority of its French territories, culminating in 1453 when Bordeaux was recaptured by the French and only Calais was left under English rule.

The Peasants' Revolt

When Edward III died, his grandson Richard II came to the throne, aged just eleven. For the next few years, England was effectively ruled in his stead by his uncle John of Gaunt, who had fought under his father Edward III in the Hundred Years Wars.

However, John was an unpopular figure (though Shakespeare gave him one of greatest patriotic speeches in *Richard II*), widely blamed for losses of French territories during the Hundred Years Wars, and for the crippling taxes needed to finance them. This, combined with dissatisfaction with the oppressive feudal system and the fear that the higher wages and privileges granted to them after the Black Death (when labour was scarce) would be withdrawn, pushed the peasantry to desperate measures.

The final straw was the Poll Tax, introduced in 1380, which taxed rich and poor alike. When officials tried to collect the tax, riots broke out all over the land, culminating in the Peasants' Revolt in 1381: an army of peasants from Kent and Essex marched on London under the leadership of Wat Tyler, Jack Straw and John Ball. Once there, Tyler's mob ran riot, capturing the Tower of London, murdering the Archbishop of Canterbury and setting fire to John of Gaunt's palace.

The young Richard II agreed to meet the leaders of the

revolt at Smithfield outside London's city walls. There was a scuffle and Wat Tyler was stabbed to death by William of Walworth, the Lord Mayor, causing uproar among the rebels. To appease them, the king promised to meet their demands but as soon as they left, he reneged on his promises and rounded up and executed the ringleaders.

The Peasants' Revolt ultimately failed, but it was the first mass uprising of common men, and a sign that the old social order was changing.

RENAISSANCE AND REFORMATION

The fifteenth and sixteenth centuries were a time of momentous change across Europe. In the seats of European learning a new cultural revival was growing, as scholars, artists and philosophers rediscovered classical texts, art and ideals. The quest for knowledge at first hand threw new light on established ideas about Church and State, leading to the religious upheaval of the Reformation and the spread of radical Protestantism in northern Europe.

THE RENAISSANCE

The Renaissance (meaning 'rebirth') was an artistic and intellectual reawakening that originated in Italy in the fourteenth century and spread to the rest of Europe. There was renewed interest in the culture and values of Ancient Greece and Rome, which combined with and enriched a school of thought that placed greater importance on the abilities of the individual, rather than on the divine or supernatural, called humanism. Scholars, clerics, writers and artists all drew on and expanded classical themes in their quest for knowledge and improvement. There are too many Renaissance luminaries to list in full but here are a few figures who pushed the boundaries of their disciplines:

Francesco Petrarch (1304–74): Italian poet and scholar, Petrarch is regarded as the 'Father of the Renaissance' and one of the earliest humanists. Prolific in his work, he was a key proponent of Greek and Roman antiquity and was instrumental in collecting and preserving classical texts.

Filippo Brunelleschi (1377–1446): The foremost architect and engineer of the Italian Renaissance. He designed the huge dome or 'duomo' of Santa Maria del Fiore in Florence and was greatly influenced by the Greek and Roman form in his work.

Johannes Gutenberg (1398–1468): German metalworker Gutenberg was the first European to use movable type and was the inventor of the mechanical printing press. His printing techniques quickly spread across Europe, and were crucial to the free circulation of ideas.

Sandro Botticelli (1444–1510): Botticelli worked mainly in Florence under the patronage of Lorenzo de' Medici. His art was inspired by the legends of Ancient Greece and Rome and his most famous pieces include *The Birth of Venus* and *Primavera* (Spring). He also helped decorate the Sistine Chapel in the Vatican.

Lorenzo de' Medici (1449–92): The Medicis were a fantastically rich Florentine banking family. Lorenzo, like his grandfather Cosimo, was a generous patron of the arts who funded, nurtured and welcomed into his court many of the key artists of the Renaissance period, including Botticelli and Michelangelo.

Leonardo da Vinci (1452–1519): Da Vinci was not only a renowned artist but also master of a dizzying array of disciplines. His best-known work of art is the *Mona Lisa*, but he was also a sculptor, a pioneer of anatomy, an inventor, an architect and an engineer, understanding the principles of flight four centuries before the invention of the first aeroplane.

Desiderius Erasmus (1466–1536): The Dutch scholar Erasmus formed the new Christian humanism, studying the original Greek New Testament, questioning the Church and rejecting the notion of predestination. In 1509 he wrote *In Praise of Folly*, criticizing the abuses of the Church and raising questions that would be influential in the Protestant Reformation (see page 62).

Niccolò Machiavelli (1469–1527): Machiavelli was a Florentine philosopher and statesman. He wrote *The Prince*, which examined how states should be governed and advised that the effective use of power may necessitate the use of unethical methods. Accused of atheism and cynicism by some, his name has become synonymous with ruthlessness and cunning.

Michelangelo di Buonarrotti (1475–1564): One of the great artists of the Renaissance, Michelangelo created two of the frescos at the Sistine Chapel, but he was also an architect and a sculptor, best known for his *Pietà* in St Peter's Basilica in Rome and the exquisite *David* commissioned for the Cathedral of Florence.

THE REFORMATION

The Reformation was a movement born from a widespread discontent with the power and corruption of the Catholic Church. It has its roots in the Renaissance when scholars like Erasmus questioned the doctrines and practices of the Church, and new translations of the Bible provoked fresh debates about Catholic doctrines. The ideas of the Reformation spread throughout northern Europe, causing Protestantism to take root in the north, while Catholicism remained entrenched in the south.

The iconic beginning to the Reformation was when Martin Luther nailed ninety-five theses to a church door in Wittenberg in 1517. Luther was an Augustine monk and professor of biblical studies at Wittenberg University and his theses protested against the excesses and hypocrisy of the Catholic Church. Luther's criticisms of the Church and his determination to question and reform its practices sparked the Protestant revolution in Germany. Luther later went on to translate the Bible into German, and attack the central Catholic doctrines of transubstantiation (the conversion of the Eucharist into the body and blood of Christ), clerical celibacy and papal supremacy.

Aided by the invention of Gutenberg's printing presses, Luther's ideas swept through Germany and Europe with great rapidity. The English Protestant William Tyndale translated the New Testament into vernacular English in 1526, but was captured and executed for heresy in the Low Countries before he could complete his translation of the Old Testament. By 1530, Sweden, Denmark and parts of Germany were receptive to Luther's reforms and proceeded to break with the Catholic Church. In 1534, Henry VIII of England also broke with Rome (see page 67), more for political convenience than out of ideological zeal, although he sought approval for the Church of England from Luther himself.

John Calvin became the second greatest reformer after Luther, although they disagreed on some points, and left a profound mark on the Protestant church. Born in France he studied for the priesthood and then

THE SPANISH INQUISITION

Special tribunals, appointed to root out and punish
heresy, were a feature of the Catholic Church since the
Middle Ages, but the most notorious and prolific was
the Spanish Inquisition, set up in 1478 by Pope Sixtus
IV, under pressure from Ferdinand and Isabella of
Spain. Though Catholicism remained entrenched in
southern Europe, the Reformation shook the Papacy
enough for the Inquisition to persecute Protestants,
as well as Jews, Muslims and other heretics (the
astronomer Galileo was summoned by the Roman
Inquisition in 1616 for arguing that the Earth revolves
around the Sun). Many of those tried had their land or
possessions confiscated, were tortured or burned alive.
The Spanish Inquisition was abolished in 1834.

law. He moved to Switzerland and it was under Calvin's
leadership that Protestantism became the dominant
religion in Geneva. It was Calvin's vision of doctrinal
revolution, later known as Calvinism, that became the
driving force behind Protestantism in western Germany,
France, the Netherlands and Scotland.

The Rise of the Tudors

One of the key moments in the Reformation was when Henry VIII broke with Rome and formed the Church of England, which his daughter Elizabeth I formalized. In so doing they laid the foundations of an institution that would survive centuries of religious quarrelling, but the Tudor accession to the English throne had been an uneasy one, marked by civil war and bloodshed.

The Wars of the Roses

Many of us have dim recollections of the Wars of the Roses, which led to the Tudor accession, and the details of this complex conflict are easily muddled (not least because almost all the protagonists were related). The Red Rose stood for the House of Lancaster and Henry VI and the White Rose for the House of York, represented by Richard Plantagenet, the third Duke of York. Both houses were branches of the Plantagenet dynasty and could claim descent from Edward III: Lancaster from his fourth son and York from his second and fifth sons (so Richard arguably had a stronger claim to the throne).

When Henry V died during the Hundred Years Wars, he left the throne to his infant son Henry VI. The young king grew up to be a weak and passive ruler, whose loss of territories in the war with France and the bad governance of favourites brought unpopularity at home.

In 1453 Henry suffered a breakdown and Richard, Duke of York, then second in line to the throne, ruled in his place. War broke out in 1455 when Henry suddenly recovered and resumed his reign. York allied with the influential Dukes of Warwick and Salisbury, and Lancaster with the Dukes of Somerset and Buckingham.

Richard had victories at St Albans and Northampton, but was killed in battle in 1460. His eldest son then crushed the Lancastrians at the Battle of Towton Moor and seized the throne as Edward IV. Edward then fell out with Warwick (nicknamed the 'Kingmaker' for his influential role) who switched allegiance to help Henry VI regain the crown briefly in 1470. Edward soon returned to the throne and had Henry imprisoned and executed.

When Edward IV died suddenly, his young son, Edward V, ruled for a few months. However, both he and his younger brother were locked up in the Tower of London 'for their own safety' by their powerful uncle, who then took to the throne as Richard III. The princes disappeared – believed to have been murdered on the orders of their uncle. (The 'Princes in the Tower' tale is a controversial one: Tudor historians would of course have been heavily biased, keen to discredit the king they had supplanted.)

Richard III's reign was beset by insurrections and in 1485 he was defeated and killed at the Battle of Bosworth Field by Henry Tudor, the last of the Lancastrians. Henry was crowned Henry VII and successfully put an end to the wars by marrying Elizabeth of York – a Tudor rose combining the red and white petals of Lancaster and York.

Henry Tudor, or Henry VII, re-established royal law and began a period of stability and peace in England. He was known as a shrewd king and by the time of his death he left his son an orderly kingdom and a vast fortune, thanks to foreign trade and the introduction of taxes.

HENRY VIII AND THE BREAK WITH ROME

Henry VIII (1491–1547) succeeded to the English throne in 1509 at the age of eighteen, a well-educated and ambitious young man with an appetite for pleasure. In the same year, he married his brother Arthur's widow, Catherine of Aragon, a partnership that was to last for many years. In 1515 the new Cardinal Wolsey was appointed Henry's chief minister and adviser. Wolsey largely organized Henry's wars, with a victorious invasion of northern France in 1513 and, in the same year, the quashing at Flodden Field of an attempted invasion by Henry's brother-in-law James IV of Scotland.

In 1518 Wolsey secured the London Treaty, a peace agreement with France, the Holy Roman Empire, the Papacy, Spain, Burgundy and the Netherlands. Wolsey also set up a meeting known as the 'Field of the Cloth of Gold' between Henry and Francis I of France in 1520, so named because each young king tried to outdo the other with dazzling pageantry and their magnificent court.

The King's Great Matter

By 1526, Henry still had no male heir and had fallen for the courtier Anne Boleyn. Convinced that his marriage to his brother's widow had been blighted by God, Henry applied to Pope Clement VII for an annulment. When the Pope refused, a crisis over the 'King's Great Matter' ensued. Cardinal Wolsey fell from grace over this issue, as did his successor Thomas More. Thomas Cromwell, a lawyer of humble origins but piercing intellect, then took over as Henry's chief adviser.

The Act of Supremacy

It was Thomas Cromwell who assisted Henry in passing the momentous laws, culminating with the Act of Supremacy in 1534, which severed the English Church from Rome and made Henry its Supreme Head. Thomas More, as Lord Chancellor, refused to sign the act and was dispatched to the executioner's block – making him a martyr of the Catholic Church, who, for his fidelity to conscience, made him a saint 400 years later.

Absolved from papal authority, Henry pressed on with his divorce from Catherine (which was secured in 1533) and implemented a series of measures to limit the power of the Church.

HENRY VIII'S WIVES

Catherine of Aragon (Q. 1509–33): Widow of Henry's brother Arthur. Henry's marriage to Catherine bore one child, Mary, and ended in divorce.

Anne Boleyn (Q. 1533–6): A courtier of Henry, Anne bore Henry a daughter, Elizabeth, but still no son. Henry had Anne executed on charges of adultery.

Jane Seymour (Q. 1536–7): Jane produced a male heir, the future Edward VI, but died two weeks later.

Anne of Cleves (Q. Jan 1540–July 1540): Henry claimed that the marriage was never consummated. They divorced six months later.

Catherine Howard (Q. 1540–1): Catherine married Henry immediately after the annulment of his previous marriage. Accused of adultery, she was executed in 1541.

Catherine Parr (Q. 1543–7): Twice- married Parr became Henry's wife until his death in 1547. She went on to marry for a fourth time.

Following his break with Rome, Henry recognized the need to assert his authority in the Catholic countries of Wales and Ireland. In 1536, Henry united Wales and England and imposed English law on the Welsh. In 1541 he declared himself 'King of Ireland', in place of the title 'Lord of Ireland', and the Crown of Ireland Act in 1542 established a personal union between the crowns, stating that whoever became king of England would also become the king of

THE FALL OF THOMAS CROMWELL

Having successfully presided over the king's divorce and break with Rome, Cromwell fell from favour when he arranged Henry's fourth marriage to Anne of Cleves. He probably knew his days were numbered after Henry shouted 'I like her not!' after their first meeting. So, following in the footsteps of so many of Henry's advisers, Cromwell was executed on charges of treason in 1540, after which his head was apparently boiled and set upon a spike at London Bridge. Henry is said to have later regretted his actions, believing Cromwell to have been one of his most faithful servants.

MARY I (1516–58)

In 1553, Mary I succeeded the Protestant Lady Jane Grey (great-granddaughter of Henry VII), who reigned for just nine days after the six-year reign of Edward VI. Mary initially received widespread support, particularly from the great number of English Catholics. However, her unpopular decision to marry the future king of Spain, Philip II, provoked Wyatt's Rebellion in 1554, named after its leader Sir Thomas Wyatt who said the marriage would turn England into a 'cockleboat towed by a Spanish galleon'.

Mary ruthlessly crushed the rebellion and executed its supporters, along with the unfortunate Lady Jane Grey and her husband. She went ahead with her marriage to Philip II and set about reversing the Protestant reforms of her father and brother. Monasteries were reopened and the laws of heresy reinstated. In the last three years of Mary's reign almost 300 Protestant heretics were burnt at the stake, earning her the nickname of 'Bloody Mary'. Mary died childless at the age of forty-two, powerless to prevent the accession of her Protestant half-sister Elizabeth.

Ireland. In reality, many Irishmen resented the claims of the English monarchy and refused to sever ties with Rome.

The Dissolution of the Monasteries

As new head of the Church, Henry set about asserting his authority by plundering its abundant resources. In sixteenth-century England, there were over 800 monasteries, accounting for a quarter of the country's land. Between 1536 and 1540, Henry's men, masterminded by Thomas Cromwell, set about demolishing these institutions, looting anything of value and selling off building material and lands to rich merchants and nobles (thereby gaining their vested interest in his Reformation). Some buildings were burnt to the ground while others were just left to crumble away.

The only voices of dissent among all this sacrilege came from Catholic gentry in the northern counties, who rose up and marched in what became known as 'The Pilgrimage of Grace' in October 1536. The protest failed, however, and Henry arrested their leaders and had them executed.

ELIZABETH I AND THE CHURCH OF ENGLAND

Daughter of Henry VIII and Anne Boleyn, Elizabeth, variously known as the 'Virgin Queen', 'Good Queen Bess' and 'Gloriana', took to the throne after the death of Mary I in 1558, and English Protestants rejoiced.

On her accession, Elizabeth swiftly set about reconciling a nation divided by religion. She picked her way through politics carefully and, after much wrangling, her first Parliament passed two great acts that brought into existence the Church of England as we know it today. The Act of Supremacy re-established the monarch as the head of the Church and the Act of Uniformity instituted the second prayer book of her half-brother Edward VI. Her aim was to introduce a moderate form of Protestantism that would appeal to English Protestants

THE VIRGIN QUEEN

Despite many eager suitors and petitions from Parliament, Elizabeth never married, although she surrounded herself with handsome courtiers. Her great favourite was her childhood friend, Robert Dudley, the Earl of Leicester, for whom Elizabeth developed a deep affection. As she grew older, her unmarried status developed into a cult of virginity, which was picked up by poets and artists who depicted her as the 'virgin queen' who was married to her kingdom and whose subjects were her children.

THE ELIZABETHAN GOLDEN AGE

The arts and culture flourished during the 'spacious times of Great Elizabeth', in Tennyson's gracious words. Poets such as Edmund Spenser and John Lyly composed great works of literature; public theatres, such as the Swan, the Rose and the Globe, began to be built under the patronage of various nobles; and dramatists such as Ben Jonson and Christopher Marlowe wrote plays that endure to this day. For us, of course, the most important writer of the period was William Shakespeare (1564–1616) whose prolific career outlasted Elizabeth and continued on into the reign of James I: between 1590 and 1613 he wrote 154 sonnets and at least 38 plays, which are still performed all around the world.

without offending Catholics too greatly.

Elizabeth declared herself an opponent of religious persecution, but even so there were heavy fines for non-attendance of Church of England services and, after 1570, executions – particularly of priests – became more common. Nonetheless, many accepted the new prayer book and most Catholics either renounced Rome or compromised their consciences to attend Protestant services.

Though indecisive over matters of foreign policy, and indeed marriage, Elizabeth knew how to control both her public image and her Parliament. She was wise enough to choose loyal and astute advisers, such as William Cecil and Francis Walsingham, who served her faithfully throughout her reign. The last fifteen years of her rule were beset with difficulties as conflicts with Spain and Ireland continued and the economy was hit with bad harvests and escalating costs of war. She died childless in 1603, the fifth and last monarch of the Tudor dynasty, though the very length of her reign served to firmly establish the Church of England.

The Plantations
In the wake of the Reformation and the Tudor claim to sovereignty over Ireland, there were waves of royalty endorsed settlement by English and Scottish Protestants in Ireland. These 'plantations' were encouraged in order to consolidate the authority of Elizabeth I and then James I. However, rebellion and civil disorder broke out in opposition to English rule and the imposition of Protestantism, notably in the Nine Years War or Tyrone's Rebellion, which broke out in 1593.

Protestant settlement accelerated in the seventeenth

century, following the mass flight of the Gaelic earls from the north of Ireland in 1607. James I claimed ownership of the land they abandoned and instigated the mass Plantation of Ulster as a means of anglicizing the population and quelling rebellion. The Plantations failed to bring the Reformation to the majority of Ireland and resulted in the displacement of thousands of landless Irish, thus shoring up more resentment against the English.

After the violent Irish rebellion of 1641, many Protestant settlers fled, but the plantations were renewed with force under Cromwell during the 1650s and again in the 1680s and 90s: in 1600, 90 per cent of the land was owned by Irish Catholics, but by 1700 they retained only 15 per cent.

Plantations had a significant impact on the demography of Ireland by creating large communities with an allegiance to Britain and Protestantism. Ulster in particular retained such an identity and the present-day partition of Ireland owes much to the pattern of plantation settlements from this period.

THE AGE OF DISCOVERY

The sixteenth century saw the beginning of the great age of European exploration. Sparked in part by the exchange of cultures that took place during the Crusades, Europeans now looked beyond the edge of the known world and wondered what other lands were yet to be discovered. New shipbuilding technology, especially the caravel, better navigation techniques and the development of cartography meant that European sailors could travel further than ever before. The expanding Ottoman Empire in the east also spurred commercial expeditions to find new sea trade routes to circumvent it in the west. Command of the sea now played an increasing role in the power-balance between European nations.

PORTUGUESE AND SPANISH EXPLORATION

With its extensive coastline and position at the south-westernmost tip of Europe, Portugal had long been a seafaring nation. Throughout the fifteenth century, expeditions led by Prince Henry the Navigator had explored the coast of Africa, as the Portuguese began to look for sea routes to Asia where they could trade gold, silver, spices and other goods. By 1498, the explorer Vasco da Gama had found a sea route to the East Indies (thus avoiding Ottoman-controlled territories on land), via the Cape of Good Hope. Between 1499 and 1502 the Italian navigator Amerigo Vespucci, under the service of the king of Portugal, made several voyages to the New World (the Americas) during which he claimed to have been the first to sight South America.

By the late fifteenth century, Spain had also joined the search for new trade routes and in 1492 the Genoese Christopher Columbus, with the support of the Spanish crown, set off across the Atlantic, reaching the Caribbean and finally central and southern America in later voyages. Further maritime exploration followed and it was under the Spanish flag that Portuguese explorer Ferdinand Magellan discovered a route to circumnavigate the globe in 1520 (via the Strait of Magellan, named in his honour).

In the sixteenth century Portugal went on to establish a string of trading posts from the coasts of Africa and Brazil to China. The Spanish also firmly established themselves in the West Indies, and central and southern America, colonizing by force in Mexico and Peru, amongst other New World colonies. By the end of the sixteenth century Spain's conquests overseas had made her the richest nation in Europe.

SOUTH AMERICAN CIVILIZATIONS

Prior to European colonization, highly developed civilizations in South America included the Aztec Empire in Mexico, which by 1500 had expanded to include as many as 6 million subjects, and the Inca Empire of western South America, which by 1525 ruled over between 8 and 10 million people and stretched across northern Ecuador, Peru, Bolivia and Chile. European diseases, such as smallpox, decimated the indigenous population, as did forced labour in the European colonies.

From the beginning of the sixteenth century, the native cultures of South America were disrupted by European colonies; first by the Portuguese who landed and colonized Brazil in 1500 and then by the Spanish, who claimed much of the continent. In 1520, Spanish soldier Hernán Cortés seized Mexico, despite fierce resistance, and slaughtered and enslaved many Aztecs in the process. The Inca Empire was similarly brought to an end when Spanish conquistador Francisco Pizarro landed on the coast in 1532, killing its emperor Atahualpa shortly after (but only once he had paid a huge ransom to the Spaniards).

ENGLISH ADVENTURERS

Early English attempts at exploration were sparked by John Cabot (an Italian navigator sailing under the English flag), who landed on the island of Newfoundland in 1497. In 1562 it was decided that England should also venture into the New World and see what it had to offer. Elizabeth gave sanction to the privateers John Hawkins and Francis Drake to engage in the work of slave trading by abducting slaves from West African towns and Spanish and Portuguese ships and transporting them to sell to colonists in the West Indies. Elizabeth later gave her blessing to piratical raids against foreign treasure ships returning from the New World, further antagonizing Spain.

From the late 1570s the idea that England should attempt to establish its own empire to rival those of Spain and Portugal became more widespread. Humphrey Gilbert led two failed attempts at colonization in North America. His first expedition in 1578 was aborted before his ships crossed the Atlantic and, at the second attempt in 1583, he made it to Newfoundland but the colonists' ships were wrecked and Gilbert himself lost at sea on the journey home.

Gilbert's half-brother, Walter Raleigh, then dispatched a fleet to the south of Newfoundland and founded a colony on the coast of present-day North Carolina, naming it Virginia in honour of Queen Elizabeth. However, he never set foot there himself and lack of supplies and foresight on

SIR WALTER RALEIGH (c.1552–1618)

After fighting against Catholic Irish rebels in Munster in 1580, Raleigh rapidly became a favourite of Elizabeth I, who granted him positions of power and influence and knighted him in 1585. In spite of this, Raleigh was an unpopular figure at court, notoriously vain and extravagant.

Raleigh fell from Elizabeth's favour in 1592 when she discovered that he had secretly married and had a son. After a period of imprisonment, he pursued fame and riches in the New World. As well as founding the colony of Virginia, he led an expedition to Venezuela in 1595 and set off to search in vain for El Dorado, the fabled city of gold in the South American interior. When Elizabeth's successor, James I, came to the throne Raleigh was tried for treason and put to death in 1618.

behalf of the settlers caused the colony to fail. Virginia was not fully established until the following century, but Raleigh and Gilbert showed what was possible and paved the way

NEW WORLD MISSIONARIES

The discovery of new lands inspired evangelical zeal among various religious groups in Europe: Roman Catholic priests joined the first Portuguese and Spanish colonists in South America, hoping to convert the heathen natives; Jesuits set up missions in South America, Canada and California, where they were joined by Franciscans; and in the seventeenth and eighteenth centuries the Church of England, as well as British Methodists and Baptists, sent out missions to New England.

for future British colonies. By 1670 there were British settlements in New England, Virginia, Antigua, Barbados, Jamaica and Honduras, with the East India Company trading from 1600 and the Hudson's Bay Company was founded in 1670 and established itself in Canada.

OTHER EARLY EMPIRES

During the 1600s, the Dutch Empire established itself as a significant naval and economic power. Founding the Dutch

East India Company in 1602, it gradually overtook Portugal in the silk and spice trade, seizing various trading posts from the Portuguese in the East Indies and Asia. Portugal also colonized Mauritius in 1638 and then in 1652 established a settlement at Cape Town, South Africa (a useful outpost for the route to Asia) before setting up colonies in the West Indies and, briefly, in Brazil. France also acquired most of its colonial empire in the 1600s, including substantial territories in North America and Canada, the Caribbean and India.

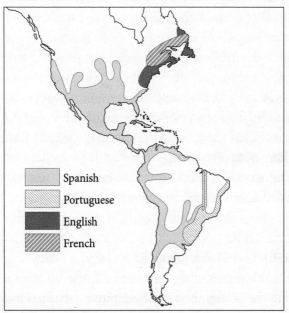

European Colonies in the Americas circa 1600

To a lesser extent, the Swedes temporarily secured outposts on the Gold Coast of Africa, and Denmark, in unison with Norway, also established the odd trading settlement on the Gold Coast, as well as in the Caribbean and India.

THE SPANISH ARMADA

From the moment Elizabeth ascended the throne, war with Spain was an ever-present threat. She managed to postpone its outbreak for twenty-seven years but by 1587 Philip II of Spain had had enough of Elizabeth's raids on Spanish ships and her support of Protestant rebels in the Spanish-controlled Netherlands. He planned to invade England with a vast fleet of ships, but a surprise raid, led by Sir Francis Drake, on the assembling fleet set back the Spanish plans for a year. Drake burned thirty of the ships before they set sail, and is said to have joked at 'singeing the king of Spain's beard'.

The Armada, consisting of about 130 heavily laden ships, finally set sail in July 1588. It was met by about 100 English ships, led by Lord Howard of Effingham and Francis Drake. Meanwhile, on land, Queen Elizabeth rallied her defence troops at Tilbury with a speech proclaiming that, although she had 'the body of a weak and feeble woman' she still had 'the heart and stomach of a king'. However, the Armada never managed to deposit

SIR FRANCIS DRAKE (c. 1540–96)

Francis Drake was feared as a pirate by foreigners, but to the English he was a hero. Having made himself a fortune plundering Spanish vessels and trading in slaves, he was then commissioned in 1577 by Elizabeth to attack Spanish colonies on America's Pacific coast. He set sail with five ships across the Atlantic, continued on to the Pacific Ocean, then the East Indies and Africa, before returning home with just his own ship, the *Golden Hind*, laden with Spanish treasure. He was the first Englishman to circumnavigate the globe and was knighted the following year by Elizabeth on board his ship. His victories against the Spanish (see opposite) further strengthened his heroic reputation at home.

its invading troops on British soil. The English ships were smaller, faster and better armed and hounded the Spanish as they sailed up the English Channel, forcing them to shelter in the port of Calais. In the night, the English sent eight blazing ships crashing into the enemy fleet, driving the Spaniards out into the North Sea. There they were harried up the east coast of England, round the northern tip of Scotland and into the Atlantic. They aimed to return to Spain via the west coast of Ireland, but much of the Spanish fleet was lost or shipwrecked in the violent North Atlantic gales.

Only sixty ships are recorded to have made it back to Spain and perhaps 15,000 Spanish sailors lost their lives, while the English lost only a handful in battle. Though it was the bad weather that ultimately scuppered the invasion, the defeat of the Spanish Armada was celebrated as the greatest English victory since Agincourt (see page 56).

RELIGIOUS FREEDOM

Many Europeans settled in the New World in the hope they could practise their religion without fear of persecution. The first settlers from Spain and Portugal were required to be Roman Catholic (as enforced by the Spanish Inquisition, which later held jurisdiction over the Spanish colonies). Many British and Dutch settlers came from varied Nonconformist backgrounds, some belonging to religious sects formed during the turmoil of the Protestant Reformation.

These settlers included English Puritans who migrated to New England (see opposite); Dutch Calvinists who settled in North America (founding New Amsterdam, which later became New York) and South Africa (where they became known as the Boers); French Huguenots, driven out from France in the late 1600s, who settled in North America and the Cape of Good Hope; British Quakers who later in the 1600s settled in Pennsylvania, along with other Baptists and German and Swiss Protestants; and Spanish and Portuguese Jews, who settled in Dutch Brazil in the 1650s but fled to North America when it was taken over by the Portuguese, joining other Jews fleeing persecution in Europe, who then established communities around New York and Rhode Island.

The Pilgrim Fathers and the *Mayflower*

In September 1620 a group of about a hundred colonists set sail from Plymouth to North America on board HMS *Mayflower*. Later called the Pilgrim Fathers, many of the colonists were fleeing religious persecution in England, and about a third of them were Separatist Puritans who had originally emigrated to the Netherlands but now wished to settle in America. The London Virginia Company, which had established the first English colony at Jamestown in 1607, gave them a licence to settle in the New World colony of Virginia.

However, rough seas pushed the *Mayflower* off-course and she landed further north, at Cape Cod. The settlers who survived the voyage were forced to establish an isolated settlement at New Plymouth, in modern-day

Massachusetts. They drew up the Mayflower Compact, which provided for a civil administration and the making of laws in the colony. Conditions were hard but roughly half the settlers managed to survive the first winter, largely through the support of the local Native Americans. They were also able to trade and make sufficient profits to buy out English shareholders. By this means they created the first self-contained, self-governing English community in America.

In 1629, more English Puritans arrived and the Massachusetts Bay Colony prospered. A wave of migration to the New World had begun and by the time of the civil wars in England, the colonies of North America were firmly established.

THE AGE OF REASON AND REVOLUTION

The seventeenth and eighteenth centuries were characterized by clashes of ideology: between monarch and parliament, state and the individual, and across the religious divide between Protestants and Catholics. In Britain, bitter civil war ultimately led to drastic constitutional overhaul, while later revolutions in America and France resulted in the creation of the United States of America and the French Republic. Revolutionary ideals in both nations were, in part, fed by the eighteenth-century school of thought known as the Enlightenment, which championed reason and the rights of the individual. At the same time, the global economy was invigorated by the Agricultural and Industrial Revolutions, which gathered pace first in Britain and then across the rest of the world.

JAMES I AND THE UNION OF CROWNS

In England the only son of the Catholic Mary Queen of Scots, James Stuart succeeded the childless Elizabeth I in 1603. James was a Protestant and, like Elizabeth, he had sought to keep the peace between Protestants and Catholics during his reign as James VI in Scotland,

THE THIRTY YEARS WAR (1618–48)

Fought mainly in Germany, the Thirty Years War was sparked by a revolt in Bohemia against the Habsburg Holy Roman Emperor Ferdinand II. The war quickly drew in other nations, including Denmark and Sweden, and became a struggle for power in Europe. In 1635 France entered the fray, fearful of Habsburg domination. Peace was concluded in the Treaty of Westphalia in 1648, although the Franco-Spanish war continued until 1659. France became the dominant power in Europe and the Holy Roman Empire lost importance within the context of Austrian and Prussian rivalries.

and barely complained when Elizabeth had his mother executed in 1567.

When he took to the English throne he was given a warm welcome, but soon made himself unpopular by surrounding himself with Scottish courtiers and by his uncompromising belief in the Divine Right of Kings. James firmly believed that it was his God-given right to rule – and, more, that as king he was God's representative on Earth. Such absolutism created conflict with anyone

THE GUNPOWDER PLOT (1605)

Catholics quickly became disillusioned with James I when he proclaimed himself a committed Protestant. This led to a Catholic extremist plot to blow up the Houses of Parliament, with the king inside, and place James's nine-year-old daughter on the throne, as a puppet monarch.

On the eve of 5 November 1605, having been tipped off by a Catholic peer, soldiers discovered Guido (Guy) Fawkes, a soldier and mining engineer, in the cellars of the Houses of Parliament along with thirty-six barrels of gunpowder. Fawkes was arrested and, along with many of the other conspirators, sentenced to be hanged, drawn and quartered. Guy cheated the executioners by jumping off the gallows and breaking his neck before the next two gruesome steps could be carried out. (The 'hanging' part of the sentence was intended to be excruciating, but not fatal.)

To celebrate his survival, the king declared that his subjects should light bonfires each year on 5 November – little did he know that this was to be celebrated with such great gusto for centuries to come.

who questioned his authority – particularly with Calvinist Protestants who believed in a more contractual form of monarchy. James argued that the king should pass the laws and control parliament, not the other way around.

James's reign saw the rise of radical (or, as they were dubbed at the time, 'hot') Protestants, or Puritans, who questioned the current translations of the Bible and the ceremonies of the Elizabethan Church. James took the opportunity to commission a new translation of the Bible, but with all the revolutionary and anti-monarchical references removed. Completed in 1611, the King James Bible endured for centuries.

James I was the first monarch to push for the political union of the crowns of England and Scotland, and created the first Union 'Jack', combining the English and Scottish flags. However, the governments of both countries were hostile to the idea, and England and Scotland remained separate nations until 1707 with the establishment of Great Britain under Queen Anne (see page 102).

THE BRITISH CIVIL WARS

On the death of James I in 1625, his son Charles I came to the throne. Like his father, Charles believed in the Divine Right of Kings: this, combined with his resolve to strengthen Catholic traditions in the Anglican Church, brought him into conflict with his Parliament. This led to a civil war that drew in all sectors of society, with communities and families divided by conflicting allegiances.

Between 1629 and 1640 Charles I avoided calling Parliament and established an autocratic 'Personal Rule'. During this time he antagonized Puritans by attempting to impose a more ritualistic Anglican service, provoking fears that he wanted to reinstate Catholicism. When he tried to impose his new 'High' Anglican prayer book on the

ROUNDHEADS AND CAVALIERS

'Roundhead' was originally intended as a pejorative term for the Protestant supporters of Parliament during the British Civil Wars. It alludes to the closely cropped haircuts of the Puritans (in contrast to the courtly fashion of long ringlets favoured by the king).

'Cavalier' was the insult used by the Parliamentarians for the supporters of the king. It literally means horseman, but Shakespeare used the term 'cavaleros' (*Henry VI, Part 2*) to denote a swashbuckling and arrogant gallant, and the term came to imply vanity and frivolousness.

Presbyterian Scots in 1637, rioting and war broke out.

Charles hastily recalled Parliament in 1640 to plead for cash for the 'Bishops' War' with the Scots; known as the 'Short Parliament', it achieved little and was quickly dissolved. The 'Long Parliament' was then called in which MPs passed a bill preventing Parliament being dissolved without its own consent. John Pym and other Puritan MPs then drew up the Grand Remonstrance, a document listing the king's faults and demanding that his ministers be approved by Parliament. This was the last straw; after a fruitless attempt to arrest Pym and the other leaders, Charles left London to raise an army and declare war.

The country was divided, with much of the north, the west and Wales siding with the king while the south-east and the Royal Navy sided with Parliament. Both armies were in the tens of thousands and the first big battle, fought at Edgehill in October 1642, was largely

CROMWELL'S COMMONWEALTH

The army, frustrated with the drawn-out negotiations between king and Parliament, then occupied London and purged Parliament of opposition. Charles was found guilty of high treason by the remaining 'Rump' Parliament and beheaded in 1649.

A republic (or what some would call a military dictatorship) was established and the country was now led by the Rump Parliament under Oliver Cromwell, whose rule came to be known as the Commonwealth. Once the king was dead, Cromwell swiftly dealt with opposition to his republic in Ireland and Scotland. First his New Model Army crossed over to Ireland and massacred thousands of Irish Royalists at Drogheda and Wexford. On his return, Cromwell defeated an army of Scottish Royalists led by Charles I's son, Charles Stuart, who then fled to France.

Like Charles I before him, Cromwell struggled with Parliament, replacing the Rump in 1653 with the 'Barebone's Parliament'. It was a blatantly rigged affair and lasted only six months before a Protectorate was proclaimed in 1655. Although Cromwell refused Parliament's offer of the crown, his installation as Lord Protector (a title for life) looked suspiciously like a coronation and, after Cromwell's death in 1658, his son Richard became Lord Protector (Cromwell having changed his mind about the value of the hereditary principle).

inconclusive, with both sides claiming victory. At the first decisive battle in November at Turnham Green, the Parliamentarian forces, led by the Earl of Essex, prevented the king's army from marching to London and forced them to retreat to Oxford.

The Royalists proceeded to make gains in the north and west, but a turning point came in 1643 with Parliamentarian victories at Gloucester and Newbury. The Scottish then allied with the Parliamentarians and entered England with 20,000 troops, joining them for the bloodiest battle of the war at Marston Moor near York in 1644. The brilliant tactics of cavalry commander Oliver Cromwell, a Puritan MP and country gentleman, proved decisive and a victory for the Roundheads secured northern England.

In 1645, Cromwell restructured the parliamentary forces to form the New Model Army, led by Sir Thomas Fairfax. Regular army wages removed the need for looting, and the 'Ironsides', as they became known, were disciplined, well-trained and united by their Puritan faith. The New Model Army crushed the king's forces at Naseby and Langport. The Royalists fled and Charles surrendered to the Scots in 1646, hoping in vain for protection; in 1647 they handed him over to Parliament.

Charles escaped to the Isle of Wight but, though he persuaded the Scots to change sides, subsequent risings failed and a combined Scottish and Royalist force was defeated at Preston in 1648, marking the end of the Civil Wars.

The Restoration

Richard Cromwell failed to control either the army or Parliament and after eight months he was forced to abdicate. A group of MPs and army officers invited Charles Stuart back from France and installed him as King Charles II in 1660, marking the beginning of the Restoration period.

The monarchy was restored with much public jubilation – its popularity a reaction in part to the strictly Puritanical regime that had been imposed during the Commonwealth, when fines had been given out to people for gambling and drinking, and holidays such as Christmas and Easter (thought to be pagan in origin) were suppressed. By contrast, the 'Merrie Monarch' was a fun-loving king who reopened the theatres and encouraged science, art, music and dancing.

On accession, Charles picked his way carefully with Parliament, executing only nine Republicans and accepting parliamentary limits to his power. However, he soon clashed with MPs over matters of religion, as he sought to promote tolerance of Catholicism (and promoted Catholics among his ministers) and allied with Catholic France in the Franco-Dutch War (1672–8).

Charles's later reign was beset by anti-Catholic conspiracy theories, particularly by that of Titus Oates, a Protestant cleric who made an insincere conversion to Catholicism. In 1678 Oates claimed that there was a Popish plot to kill the king and slaughter Protestants. This proved to be entirely fictitious, but it provoked anti-Catholic hysteria and many innocent Catholics were arrested or killed. The plot also led to the attempt by some MPs to stop Charles's Catholic brother James succeeding to the throne. This created such division among MPs that they formed two political parties: the Whigs who were against the accession of James and the Tories who supported him: effectively a 'country' party and a 'court' party.

The Great Plague and the Fire of London

The Great Plague flared up in London in the summer of 1665, exacerbated by the heat and poor sanitation and killing as much as a fifth of the population of the city. It is thought to have come from the Netherlands, Amsterdam having been hit the previous year, and was the last wave of the Black Death that had hit Europe in the fourteenth century (see page 53). The Lord Mayor ordered that anyone who showed symptoms was to be locked in their houses with their families, thereby mortally endangering family members.

Hot on the heels of the plague was the Great Fire, which devastated London in the late summer of 1666. It began in a bakery in Pudding Lane and spread quickly, fanned by an east wind and fuelled by the city's tightly-packed timbered buildings. It swiftly destroyed much of the old city, engulfing St Paul's Cathedral, the stones of which

THE REBUILDING OF ST PAUL'S

The Norman Cathedral of St Paul's was in a state of near ruin before the Great Fire delivered the last blow and the architect Christopher Wren already had designs for a replacement in hand. Built between 1675 and 1711, it was Wren's masterpiece and for a time the great dome of St Paul dominated the city's skyline, and was a symbol of pride for Londoners, particularly during the Blitz (see page 169), when it miraculously escaped obliteration.

'flew like grenados' while the pavements glowed with 'fiery redness', as diarist John Evelyn wrote at the time.

After four days the fire had burnt itself out: it had destroyed 13,200 homes, though only about six people perished, and the fire had destroyed many of London's unsanitary slums.

MP and naval administrator Samuel Pepys provided a vivid account of the plague and the fire of London in his diary, written between 1660 and 1669. In it he wrote about his private life and the major public events of the Restoration period, including the coronation of Charles II.

The Glorious Revolution

When Charles II died in 1685 with no legitimate heir, his Catholic brother James succeeded him as James II, to the consternation of the largely Protestant Parliament. Revolution was set in motion when James II fathered a son in 1688, making the threat of a Catholic dynasty an imminent reality.

THE BILL OF RIGHTS (1689)

The Bill of Rights is one of the most important documents in British political history. It was the precursor to the United States Bill of Rights and influenced later constitutional law around the world. It laid out certain basic rights of all Englishmen living under a constitutional monarchy. These included freedom from royal interference with the law, freedom from taxation by Royal Prerogative, and freedom of speech and debates. As a prelude to the 1701 Act of Settlement, the Bill of Rights also stipulated that Roman Catholics should be excluded from the crown.

THE WAR OF THE SPANISH SUCCESSION (1701–13)

The War of the Spanish Succession was a conflict that arose following the death of the Spanish Habsburg king, Charles II. With no natural heir, he had bequeathed his territories to Philip, duc d'Anjou, who also happened to be in line to the French throne. The terrible prospect of a union between France and Spain caused shock waves across Europe, and in a bid to prevent it, an alliance was formed in 1701 between the English, the Dutch and most of the German princes in support of an Austrian claim to the Spanish Empire.

Fighting took place mainly in Europe but also in North America where the English fought against the French in 'Queen Anne's War' between 1702 and 1713. The wars ended with the Treaty of Utrecht in 1713, which recognized Philip of Anjou as Philip V of Spain but removed him from the French line of succession. Britain emerged more powerful, gaining considerable territory in North America, as well as the right to ship slaves to the Spanish colonies.

Already troubled by the king's Catholicism and his alliance with France, leading politicians of both the Whig and Tory parties invited Charles II's Protestant daughter Mary and her husband William of Orange to England. William arrived with his Dutch army, thanks, some claimed, to the 'Protestant wind', and after facing some fierce resistance in Scotland and Ireland, William and Mary deposed James II and were crowned joint monarchs in 1689. Parliament affirmed its authority with the Bill of Rights, a document that established England as a constitutional monarchy, making the Glorious Revolution far more definitive than Cromwell's Commonwealth.

William III and Mary II ruled as joint monarchs until Mary's death, though Mary often ruled alone when William was abroad, suppressing the Jacobite rebellions and fighting wars against France and the Netherlands. When Mary died, William became sole monarch and, with no living offspring, the crown passed to Mary's younger sister Anne following William's death in 1702.

THE ACTS OF UNION AND THE JACOBITE CAUSE

Queen Anne became the last of the Stuart monarchs in 1702. When it became apparent she would leave no male heir a crisis over succession led to the Act of Settlement in 1701, which barred Catholics from the throne (thus excluding the Stuart Pretenders), or indeed anyone who might marry a Catholic. Perhaps the most important legacy of Anne's rule was the Acts of Union in 1707 which merged England and Scotland as one sovereign state. While England and Scotland had shared the same monarch since the accession of James I in 1603, the two countries were now, in the phrase of the Acts 'one united kingdom by the name of Great Britain'. It wasn't until 1801 that the second Act of Union (partly provoked by the Irish Rebellion of 1798 – see page 112) proclaimed the United Kingdom of Great Britain and Ireland.

Jacobite Rebellions

The first Jacobite rebellion had been a reaction to James II's deposition (Jacobite meaning supporter of James), but had little popular support and quickly fizzled out. However, the cause revived with the unpopularity of William III. Several economic and political disasters (one being a failed attempt at creating a Scottish colony in Panama) led many to flock to the Jacobite cause. The Acts of Union under Queen Anne further stirred nationalist opinion and the French added their support, sending James II's son, James Stuart (also known as the Old Pretender), to Scotland with an invasion force in 1708 but they turned back when they realized the Royal Navy was already lying in wait.

Two more major Jacobite rebellions were to surface over the next fifty years – fuelled mainly by high taxes and inadequate Scottish representation in Parliament. The first, in 1715, sought to overthrow the Hanoverian George I. It posed a serious threat to the Union and saw Catholics from Lancashire also taking up arms. However, poor leadership led to the rebels' defeat and the Old Pretender fled back to France.

The second, in 1745, aimed to install James Stuart's son Charles (Bonnie Prince Charlie, also known as the Young Pretender) on the throne in place of George II. The Young Pretender arrived on Scottish shores to a groundswell of popular support, allowing him to invade England as far as Derby before being forced to retreat.

The rebellion culminated in defeat at Battle of Culloden, which earned the Hanoverian commander the nickname 'Butcher Cumberland' for his merciless slaughter of the Highland troops. The Jacobite cause was routed and, though he retained a few diehard supporters, Bonnie Prince Charlie died a heavy drinker in exile.

THE ENLIGHTENMENT

The Enlightenment or Age of Reason was a cultural and philosophical movement underpinned by a belief in the power of reason. It gained momentum during the eighteenth century, as Enlightenment thinkers questioned established institutions and the accepted social order and attacked both superstition and the Church itself as an enemy of reason. As a movement, it championed secular values and paved the way for the democracy and liberal capitalism of modern society. Its theories were to influence scientific theory, politics, law, economics and the arts, and formed the intellectual basis for the French and American Revolutions.

Writers and philosophers, such as Voltaire and Rousseau in France, began to apply Enlightenment principles to society, making the case that all people are equal. In Britain, too, Enlightenment ideals were spreading: the philosophers Adam Smith and David Hume advocated empiricism and economic liberalism, social reformer Jeremy Bentham argued for the abolition of slavery, and the political writer Thomas Paine wrote in support of American independence and the French Revolution. In Scotland, important scientific advances were made in chemistry, geology, medicine and economics.

THE AMERICAN WAR OF INDEPENDENCE

Relations between Britain and its American colonies had deteriorated during the eighteenth century, largely through colonial resentment at the commercial policies of Britain and lack of representation at Westminster. A conflict over taxation culminated in the Boston Tea Party in 1773, when protesting colonists dumped three shiploads of tea into Boston Harbour. Protest developed into armed resistance at Concord and Lexington in 1775 and finally full-scale war. King George III refused to compromise over taxes or address the colonists' grievances, and public sentiment favoured independence (partly fuelled by Thomas Paine's pamphlet 'Common Sense'). With no hope of a peaceful resolution, the Second Continental Congress drew up the Declaration of Independence on 4 July 1776.

> 'These united Colonies are, and of Right ought to be Free and Independent States, that they are Absolved from all Allegiance to the British crown, and that all political connection between them and the State of Great Britain, is and ought to be totally dissolved.'
>
> DECLARATION OF INDEPENDENCE (1776)

The Declaration gave moral justification for the war with Britain and unified the American colonies under one cause. But Britain was not prepared to concede without a fight, and the war continued for another five years. Despite outnumbering the rebels, Britain suffered from problems of supply (each soldier required a third of a ton of food to be transported every year), a hostile population, lack of local knowledge and guerrilla tactics.

In 1778, the Continental Congress formed an alliance

GEORGE WASHINGTON (1732–99)

Washington was born the son of a Virginia planter and served in the British army before leading the American forces to independence. He became the first president of the United States – and for this reason, as well as his involvement in the Revolutionary War, he is often referred to as the 'father of the nation'. He served for two terms as US president, from 1789 to 1799, and was described by Congressman Henry Lee as, 'first in war, first in peace and first in the hearts of his countrymen'.

with France, and over the next two years Spain and the Dutch Republic also declared war on Britain during which British forces were distracted by the conflict in Minorca and Gibraltar and in the East and West Indies. A Franco-American force won the final major battle at Yorktown, Virginia in 1781. After two years of negotiation, the 1783 Treaty of Paris finally concluded Britain's capitulation and recognized the independence of the United States of America. The once dismissed 'Vagabond Army of Ragamuffins' had triumphed.

THE WAR OF 1812

Some thirty years after the Wars of Independence, hostilities between Britain and the United States broke out once more, due to trade blockades between France and America during the Napoleonic Wars (see page 121). Britain also began seizing thousands of sailors from American merchant ships in the Atlantic for enlistment into the British navy.

War was declared in June 1812: American warships won a series of engagements but were unable to break up the British blockade. There were a series of large inconclusive battles across America, the most famous being the British raids on Chesapeake Bay which resulted in the burning of the President's Mansion in Washington DC (known as the 'White House' from 1901).

When Britain defeated France in the Napoleonic Wars, trade restrictions were lifted and the two sides signed a peace treaty in Belgium on Christmas Eve 1814 (though news did not reach America until February 1815, by which time the Americans had defeated the British at New Orleans, resulting in 2,000 British casualties).

THE FRENCH REVOLUTION

The French Revolution changed the face of Europe as monarchy and the established order of the Ancien Régime were swept away in favour of a government based on the Enlightenment principles of citizenship and equality. It is also one of the most violent and bloody chapters in France's history.

France had been gripped by a financial crisis caused by Louis XVI's involvement in the Seven Years War (see page 110) and his support of the colonists in the American War of Independence. High bread prices and unemployment had led to famine and crippling poverty among much of the population, who resented the privileges and ostentatious consumption of the nobility.

In May 1789, the financial crisis led to the calling of the Estates-General, a representative assembly organized into three estates: the Church, the nobility and the Third Estate (everybody else). When it became clear that the clergy and nobility could outvote the Third Estate, its bourgeois leaders began a struggle for equal rights.

In June 1789 the Third Estate reconvened and declared itself the National Assembly, an assembly of the 'people', not of the estates. The monarchy and nobility attempted to dissolve the National Assembly, which was prevented by the *sans-culottes*, the artisans and workers of Paris, who rose up and attacked the Bastille on 14 July. The king consequently lost control of Paris and the countryside when a series of peasant rebellions, known as the Great Fear, took hold over much of France in a summer of panic between July and August 1789.

The National Assembly then passed the August Decrees, abolishing noble privilege, and published the

THE SEVEN YEARS WAR (1756–63)

The Seven Years War drew in all the major powers of Europe and involved two linked conflicts: the struggle for supremacy in Germany between Austria and Prussia, and colonial rivalry between Britain and France. Prussia fought mainly on European soil against the combined forces of Russia, France, Austria and Sweden, while her ally Britain clashed with France over colonial territories in North America, Africa and India. The Treaties of Paris and Hubertusburg concluded the war in 1763. Their terms reduced France's imperial influence, increased Prussia's status within central Europe and established Britain as the leading colonial power, gaining India and North America, including French Canada.

ABOLITION OF THE FRENCH MONARCHY

In 1792, war with Austria, which then led to a series of French Revolutionary Wars (see page 121), brought more radical policies. The king and his Austrian Queen Marie Antoinette were suspected of backing an Austrian victory. The monarchy was abolished and the king and queen tried and executed in 1793.

Declaration of the Rights of Man and of the Citizen, a proclamation of human rights and civic equality modelled on the Declaration of Independence of the United States.

Between 1789 and 1791 the Constituent Assembly proceeded to implement a number of radical reforms. These included legislation that radically limited the power of the Catholic Church in France: abolishing its rights to impose tithes, appropriating its property, dissolving religious orders and severing its ties with the Pope. The Church was now a wing of the State. For the first time counter-revolution received mass support and the king fled to Varennes as demands for a republic were voiced.

THE IRISH REBELLION OF 1798

Roused in part by the success of the American and French Revolutions, a group called the United Irishmen staged an uprising in 1798, with the aim of securing independence from England. The rebellion, which became a popular one against landlords and Protestants, ultimately failed – in spite of military assistance from Revolutionary France – and was brutally quashed by the British army. The conflict was marked by its violence and brutality, involving massacres, torture and rape, and leaving between 30,000 and 40,000 Irish dead.

While France suffered from high inflation, revolts and defeat by the Austrians, the Convention set up the Revolutionary Tribunal and the Committee of Public Safety, which became dominated by the more radical 'Jacobins' and their leader Maximilien Robespierre. The committee implemented the 'Great Terror' between September 1793 and July 1794 to crush any resistance to the regime; Robespierre, its key driving force, called it 'justice implacable'. Real or imagined enemies of the regime were executed and it is estimated that around 50,000 people died (most of them peasants or urban workers) either on the guillotine, in counter-revolutionary clashes or in jail.

Dissent grew among the Jacobins, and Robespierre, along with twelve others, was sent to the guillotine without trial in July 1794, bringing an end to the Terror. There were several different forms of administration before the *coup d'état* of Brumaire in 1799, which then established the consulate of Napoleon Bonaparte (see page 122).

THE AGRICULTURAL AND INDUSTRIAL REVOLUTIONS

In Britain, a revolution of a different kind was set in motion during the latter half of the 1700s, spurred less by bloodshed and war than by economic and social forces, but which nonetheless transformed a mostly rural society into a modern, urbanized, industrial power. The effects of the Agricultural and Industrial Revolutions later spread across Europe and America, causing enormous social change and economic growth, along with the rise of a powerful new middle class.

The Agricultural Revolution

For many centuries, families had farmed their land on narrow strips in open fields belonging to wealthy landowners (see page 46). The enclosure of this land, a process by which the landlords took over the strips and made them into larger, more productive fields, increased dramatically in the eighteenth century, with some landowners also taking over common land. Government legislation, culminating in the General Enclosure Act of 1801, led to large-scale reform resulting in the enclosure of a quarter of England's farmland. As enclosed fields were grouped together to form larger farms, many rural workers and smaller landlords were forced to seek employment elsewhere.

Key Developments of the Agricultural Revolution:

• The Four-Field Crop Rotation System: A Dutch system introduced by Viscount 'Turnip' Townshend in the 1730s whereby, instead of fields being left fallow every third year in order to rest the soil, crops like turnips or clover that improved the fertility of the soil were grown, providing winter food for livestock.

• The Seed Drill: A mechanical seeder developed by Jethro Tull in 1701, which carefully planted seeds into the soil instead of scattering them across the surface by hand, ensuring a better rate of germination and a higher crop yield.

• Selective breeding: Robert Bakewell and Thomas Coke began to select the healthiest, most productive animals from which to breed and experimented by combining different breeds. The result was an increase in market value of the livestock and a greater yield of produce.

THE HIGHLAND CLEARANCES

Changes in farming methods also led to the Highland Clearances of the late eighteenth and early nineteenth centuries, when Scottish landowners evicted whole communities from their land to make way for more lucrative sheep farms or grouse hunting. Some were forced to move to towns for employment while many others emigrated, principally to America. The forced evictions were so successful that, in some areas, hardly any trace of Highland settlement has survived.

The Industrial Revolution

As farming methods improved and overseas trade grew, Britain's manufacturing also underwent major transition from a rural economy based on manual labour to an urban, mechanized one.

A stable government, the availability of capital, as well as crucial reserves of coal and iron ore all ensured that

THE COTTAGE INDUSTRY

The cottage industry, the manufacture of products at home, was a common feature of eighteenth-century Britain. Its workforce consisted of the great mass of rural labourers and their families who needed to earn additional income, as well as those evicted by the enclosures. Many were involved in cloth-making, a flourishing industry in Britain and a key driving force of the Industrial Revolution. The whole family was often involved in the cloth-making process and the final woven cloth would then be sold to local clothiers. However, by the end of the century, the cottage industry had been largely replaced by mechanized factories made possible by new developments in technology.

Britain was at the forefront of the Industrial Revolution, but it soon spread to Europe and America in the nineteenth century.

Key Developments of the Industrial Revolution:

- The Flying Shuttle: Patented by John Kay in 1733, it enabled the weaver to throw the shuttle across the loom and back again with one hand.

- The Spinning Jenny: Invented by James Hargreaves in 1764, this new spinning wheel enabled operators to spin eight threads at once.

- Water power: In 1769, Richard Arkwright designed a water-powered spinning machine and in 1785 Edmund Cartwright made the first water-powered loom, which was later driven by steam.

- Sheet iron: In 1709, Abraham Darby worked out how to produce sheet iron from coke (a pure form of coal). Iron goods could be now be produced on a much bigger scale. Most industrial machines, steam engines, and later the railway, were all made from iron, making it a vital element of the Industrial Revolution.

- The steam engine: The industrial steam engine was improved and developed by James Watt (after whom the unit of power is named). By 1800 there were over 500 of Watt's engines in Britain's mines, mills and factories. His engine made possible the construction of new factories that could run all year round away from water sources.

The Industrial Revolution saw the rise of large-scale factories and increasing urbanization as traditional craftsmen, labourers and their families migrated from rural areas to the growing towns and cities in search of work. In the nineteenth century, small market towns grew quickly into great factory-dominated cities, such as Birmingham, Liverpool and Manchester (nicknamed 'Cottonopolis' after its proliferation of cotton mills).

Industrial workers generally earned a tiny wage and conditions in many of the factory towns were grim, where inadequate housing and poor sanitation often led to the spread of disease. Child labour was common, with children expected to work up to sixteen hours a day operating dangerous machinery. Factory reforms later improved working conditions and legislated against the use of child labour.

In the nineteenth century, industrialization spread to Europe, first to Belgium, and then on to the larger countries of the continent. From the 1850s, new coalfields in the Ruhr and Pas de Calais facilitated the expansion of the railway. After unification in 1871, industry spread rapidly in Germany, particularly in the steel, chemicals and electrical industries. At the same time, industrialization increased exponentially in the US, aided by its vast railway network and iron and steel-making industries, so that by 1900 the US was the world's biggest industrial power.

The New Age of Transport

The process of industrialization in Britain went hand-in-hand with improvements to its transport system. Raw goods and finished products needed to be transported, and new developments in materials and engineering enabled thousands of miles of roads, canals and railway tracks to be built.

- Roads: From around 1720 newly established turnpike trusts built and maintained thousands of miles of new roads, for which they collected a toll from gatehouses built at either end of the road (many of which can still be seen today). The Scotsman John McAdam invented a process for building harder, more weatherproof roads using a layer of small stones coated with tar (called 'tarmacadam' or 'tarmac' in his honour).

• Canals: A vast network of canals was also built across Britain. A single canal horse could pull a load ten times the weight of that on a cart, and at a faster pace. One of the first canals was constructed by the engineer James Brindley in 1759 and over the next fifty years a network of 3,700 miles of canals were built, linking manufacturing centres in the Midlands and the north with seaports and London.

• Railways: In 1804 Richard Trevithick produced the first steam-powered train. George Stephenson then improved the design with the 'Rocket' steam train, and was responsible for the world's first passenger steam railway built in 1825. Construction of public railways linking cities with towns began in the 1830s, and by 1855 thousands of miles of railway tracks snaked across Britain. Thereafter railways were built across the world with the US completing the first transcontintenal railroad, linking the Atlantic with the Pacific, in 1869, and by the end of the century railway networks reached across Europe, the US, Canada and some parts of Russia.

THE AGE OF EMPIRE

The industrial revolution in turn led to further advances in technology and science as well as a period of expansionism as European nations looked overseas for raw material to feed their rapidly growing industry. Revolutionary France pursued an aggressive expansionist policy under Napoleon. At the same time, the newly independent United States extended further west towards the Pacific as European powers carved up a great mass of colonies overseas, with Britain in particular building a vast empire. European nations fought near-constant colonial conflicts as the newly unified empire of Germany emerged as a major power in Europe. The resulting tensions would erupt in the First World War.

THE FRENCH REVOLUTIONARY AND NAPOLEONIC WARS

In Europe, a series of wars raged in the late eighteenth and early nineteenth centuries as various European coalitions fought against the French: first in the French Revolutionary Wars (1792–1802), when Austria, Britain, Prussia and others initially sought to restore Louis XVI to power, followed by the Napoleonic Wars (1803–15) to limit the aggressive expansion of Napoleon Bonaparte.

HEROES OF THE NAPOLEONIC WARS

Napoleon Bonaparte (1769–1821): One of the greatest military leaders in history, Napoleon began his military career at the age of fourteen, took over the leadership of France in the military coup of 1799 and by 1804 was named the 'Emperor of the French'. Under his rule, France became a dominant power in Europe. The Battle of Waterloo ended Napoleon's time in power, and he died in imprisonment.

Horatio Nelson, First Viscount Nelson, Duke of Bronte (1758–1805): Born the son of a county parson, Horatio Nelson entered the navy at the age of twelve, was captain by the age of twenty and rear admiral before he was forty. He won his greatest victory over the French at the Battle of Trafalgar in 1805, where he died from his wounds. He was the first commoner ever to receive a state funeral.

Arthur Wellesley, First Duke of Wellington (1769–1852): Born to impoverished Irish nobility, Wellesley left Ireland to join the army, gaining experience in the last few years of the French Revolutionary Wars, rising to commander of the British forces in the Peninsular War of 1812. After his invasion of France in 1814, he was granted a dukedom and the following year won his great victory at Waterloo (according to him 'the nearest run thing you ever saw in your life'). He later served as prime minister and when he died he was given a state funeral, as Nelson before him.

Both wars raged throughout Europe but were also fought in the Middle East, southern Africa and the Caribbean, as the French gained and then lost a vast empire.

Napoleon secured a series of decisive victories against the Austrians in northern Italy in 1796, but his fleet suffered defeat by the English under Admiral Nelson at Aboukir Bay in Egypt in 1798. The British and French signed a peace agreement at Amiens in 1802. Britain renewed the war a year later, in response to Napoleon's occupation of Malta. In 1805, Nelson destroyed the combined Spanish and French fleet at the Battle of Trafalgar, during which he was mortally wounded. In the same year, Napoleon defeated the emperors of Austria and Russia at the Battle of Austerlitz. Victory in the Napoleonic Wars led to the expansion of French influence throughout much of western Europe (excluding Britain) and into Poland.

Napoleon next set his sights on Spain, but his invasion of the Iberian Peninsula was repelled by Spain, Portugal and Britain during the Peninsular War in 1811. Napoleon's Moscow campaign in 1812 was an even worse disaster, his army decimated by a bitter Russian winter, leading to the death of nearly half a million men (the retreat was commemorated by Tchaikovsky in his *1812 Overture*). After another defeat for the French at Leipzig, Wellington invaded France in 1814: Napoleon was forced to abdicate and was imprisoned on the island of Elba.

Napoleon escaped from Elba in 1815 and retook power in France for a brief period, known as the Hundred Days, but was finally defeated by the Duke of Wellington, aided by the Prussians, at the Battle of Waterloo. Napoleon was banished well out of harm's way to Saint Helena in the South Atlantic, the Spanish Empire weakened and Britain emerged as a leading world power and mistress of the seas.

THE BRITISH EMPIRE

The British Empire reached its peak during the Victorian era, covering, at its greatest extent, one quarter of the world's land mass – the largest empire ever known.

While the empire prospered abroad, the political system as we now know it developed at home. Power shifted between two main political parties: the Tories (or

QUEEN VICTORIA (1819–1901)

Victoria came to the throne at the age of eighteen in 1837, and went on to rule for sixty-three years. She is the second-longest-serving British monarch, as well as the one who presided over the greatest number of colonies. In 1840 she married Albert of Saxe-Coburg-Gotha and together they had nine children. When Albert died in 1861, Victoria withdrew into a prolonged period of mourning and continued to wear black for the rest of her life. She died at the age of eighty-one and was buried alongside Albert at Frogmore, near Windsor.

Conservatives) and the Whigs (who would later form the core of the Victorian Liberal Party). The 1832 Great Reform Act extended the vote to some 300,000 middle-class subjects (though the majority of the working class were still excluded, leading to the Chartist campaigning of 1838–50) and later Acts further extended the franchise. The Independent Labour Party was formed during a split from the Liberals in 1893.

Britain's new technology, prosperity and shipbuilding

VICTORIAN INNOVATORS

Isambard Kingdom Brunel (1806–59): Brillant
engineer and designer Brunel constructed over 1000
miles of railway, 125 bridges and three great ships:
his ship the SS *Great Western* sailed from Bristol to
New York in 1838 and was the first steam ship to
make regular Atlantic crossings.

Charles Darwin (1809–82): In 1831 Darwin joined
a surveying expedition to South America aboard
HMS *Beagle*. Over the course of the journey he
became a keen scientist and naturalist, publishing
his great theory of evolution by natural selection,
The Origin of Species, in 1859.

**Joseph Swan (1828–14) and Thomas Edison
(1847–1931):** In 1878 and 1879 Swan in Britain and
Edison in America both independently invented the
electric light bulb. The Houses of Parliament and the
British Museum were the first public buildings to be lit
by electricity.

Alexander Graham Bell (1847–1922): In 1876,
the appropriately named Bell, a Scotsman living in
America, invented the telephone by using telegraph

technology to transmit the sound of voices. When demonstrated to Queen Victoria in 1878, she said it was 'rather faint'.

skills – as well as the commercial force behind enterprises such as the East India Company – ensured her early advantage in the race between European nations to obtain overseas territories, trade and resources. At the beginning of the nineteenth century, Britain already held territories overseas, including parts of Canada, Cape Colony in South Africa, Australia and New Zealand, and many West Indian islands.

After the defeat of Napoleon at Waterloo, and with a mighty navy that really did rule the waves, Britain was able to expand its imperial holdings with renewed vigour. The East India Company expanded the British Empire in Asia, including the acquisition of Singapore in 1819 and parts of Burma in 1826 (acquired in its entirety in 1886 after the Anglo-Burmese wars). In 1839 Britain secured Aden, Hong Kong in 1841 (see page 140) and after the Indian Mutiny of 1857 (see page 141) Britain took over the vast subcontinent of India. New tropical colonies were acquired during the 'Scramble for Africa' (see page 132) and in 1888 Britain installed protective

THE IRISH QUESTION

Since the Act of Union in 1801, Ireland had been part of the United Kingdom, administered by the British government in Westminster. Much of the vast rural population of Ireland lived in abject poverty, only to be devastated in 1845 when blight hit the Irish potato crop, followed by two bad harvests. The Great Famine struck and by 1852 over a million people had died. The Famine strengthened feelings of mistrust towards Britain and increased calls for independence. The Irish politician Charles Stuart Parnell ran a peaceful campaign for Home Rule (the re-establishment of an Irish Parliament responsible for internal affairs), and by 1885 Parnell's Home Rule party had eighty-six members in Parliament and had convinced then Prime Minister William Gladstone that this was the solution to the 'Irish Question'. Gladstone twice tried to pass an Irish Home Rule Bill but was defeated by politicians who feared it might have a knock-on effect across the empire. Home Rule wasn't established for southern Ireland until the following century (see page 158).

troops on the strategically important Suez Canal (which was not owned or controlled by any one state).

OTHER EUROPEAN EMPIRES

In the nineteenth century, the French Empire grew into the second biggest colonial power after Britain. In 1830 the French began their conquest of Algeria, in 1881 secured Tunisia as a protectorate and later acquired territories in Asia to form French Indochina in 1887. French enclaves were also secured in parts of China and by end of the 1800s the French had control of much of western, northern and central Africa.

The Spanish Empire effectively ended during the nineteenth century, losing all her American territories during the Napoleonic Wars and the Spanish–American Wars of Independence: by the end of the century Spain retained only her African territories in a small part of Morocco, Equatorial Guinea and Western Sahara. Portugal similarly lost its South American settlements, later focusing on its bases in Africa, which included Angola and Mozambique. Late in the nineteenth century Bismarck's Germany claimed German South-West Africa, the Cameroons and German East Africa and Belgium's Leopold II set himself up as sovereign of the Congo Free State in 1876.

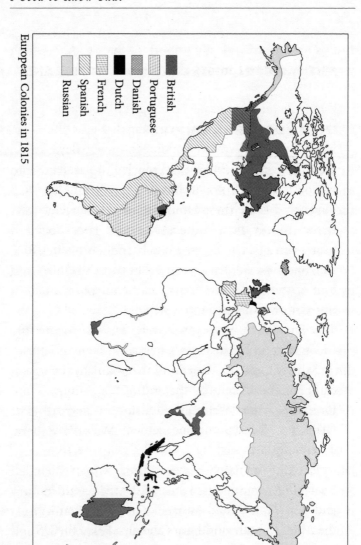

European Colonies in 1815

British
Portuguese
Danish
Dutch
French
Spanish
Russian

SETTLEMENT IN AUSTRALIA AND NEW ZEALAND

Captain James Cook sailed to the South Pacific in the late eighteenth century, mapping the coast of New Zealand in 1769 and landing in Botany Bay, Australia, in 1770. By 1788, Sydney Bay, Australia, was declared the first British penal settlement. Men (and some women) were transported for a range of crimes, mostly theft. With good conduct, they could be granted a ticket of leave – and be free to obtain paid work on the condition that they never left Australia. Voluntary emigration began from the 1820s and squatter settlements, particularly in the east, led to violent conflict with the Aborigines. In 1901, Australia was declared a British Commonwealth state.

Settlers began arriving in New Zealand in the early nineteenth century, first setting up stations for seal- and whale-hunting and later establishing farms, mines and permanent settlements. British sovereignty was declared in 1840, though fierce resistance from native Maori tribes continued. New Zealand became a self-governing dominion in 1907, and New Zealand and Australian troops served with the Allies in both world wars and also aided the US in the Vietnam War.

THE SCRAMBLE FOR AFRICA

Since antiquity, North Africa has been colonized by a host of invaders, including the Greeks and Phoenicians, the Carthaginians, Romans, Vandals, and from the seventh century onwards, Arabs, who brought Islamic culture and the Arabic language to North and parts of East Africa. In the fifteenth century, Portugal and then other European nations explored much of the coastline of Africa, establishing outposts and implementing the African slave trade.

However, at the start of the nineteenth century, the vast interior of the continent (after which Joseph Conrad named his novel *The Heart of Darkness*) was still largely untouched by Europeans until missionaries and explorers ventured further. French explorer René Caillie became the first European to survive a visit to Timbuktu in 1828. Scottish Protestant missionary David Livingstone explored the Zambezi River, discovering and renaming the Victoria Falls in 1855. In 1866 he led an expedition to find the source of the Nile, his mysterious disappearance and death further sparking obsession with the African interior. John Hanning Speke and Sir Richard Burton became the first Europeans to reach Lake Tanganyika in 1858. Speke went on to reach another great lake, which he named Lake Victoria and which eventually proved to be the source of the Nile.

In the 1880s, armed with new information about Africa's untapped resources, particularly minerals and precious metals, European nations, led by Britain, France and Germany, conducted a series of military campaigns against African nations in order to seize as much land as possible (called the 'Scramble for Africa' after an 1884 conference in Berlin when European powers agreed upon the partition of the continent).

Wars raged across west, central and eastern Africa as European colonial powers fought amongst themselves as well as with African nations. Key conflicts included the Anglo-Zulu Wars of 1879, the Sudan Campaign of 1885 and the Boer Wars (1880-1 and 1899-1902), which culminated with the Treaty of Vereeniging in 1902, under which the Boer Republics became British colonies, with the promise of self-government.

By the early twentieth century, most of Africa was under European control: the French controlled territory in parts of the west, north and around the equator, the Germans and Belgians gained colonies along the Congo and in the south, the Portuguese occupied Angola and Mozambique, while Britain dominated the east from South Africa to Egypt, as well as parts of the west (comprising seventeen colonies and extending over 4 million square miles of land). Other European nations claimed what remained and only Ethiopia and Liberia remained independent states.

AMERICAN EXPANSION

As the European empires expanded, the United States established itself further into the North American continent, pushing westward towards the Pacific. Between 1850 and 1900 millions of Americans and European immigrants settled on the western plains and further west beyond the Rocky Mountains.

In 1803 the United States effectively doubled its size when it purchased the Louisiana territories from the French. By 1820, Florida, Missouri and Maine had become part of the Union and, by 1848, after conflicts with Mexico, Texas, California and New Mexico were also included.

Meanwhile the 1846 Oregon treaty with Britain led to US control of the north-west, and a Mormon settlement was established in Salt Lake City, Utah. The Gold Rush, sparked in California in 1848, brought a further influx of settlers (the 'forty-niners'), and created new towns, roads and railways, with other rushes following in the 1850s.

By the end of the Spanish-American War in 1898, the Union had purchased Alaska from the Russians, annexed Hawaii and taken control of Puerto Rico, Guam and the Philippines, all of which secured the United States' status as a major world power.

Manifest Destiny

'[It is] our manifest destiny to overspread the
continent allotted by Providence for the free
development of our yearly multiplying millions . . .'

This was a phrase used by New York editor John
O'Sullivan in 1845 to justify US control of the entire
North American continent. He wrote that no nation
should be allowed to interfere with America's territorial
expansion, its 'manifest destiny'. He initially used the
phrase to urge the annexation of Texas in 1845 but it was
soon adopted to promote the vision of US expansionism.
It evolved into an ideal and moral belief, bolstering the
divine mission of the United States to spread democracy
and freedom across the continent.

Native Americans were to feel the impact of Manifest
Destiny as it gave sanction to the US occupation of
Native American land. As armed settlers set up farms
on the western plains, Native Americans were driven
away and their buffalo massacred in the millions. Native
Americans fought back, most famously at the Battle of
the Little Bighorn in 1876 when Sioux warriors led by
Sitting Bull and Crazy Horse killed 250 US soldiers
along with their Lieutenant Colonel Custer. This came
to be known in American history as 'Custer's Last Stand'.
The US forces finally clamped down on all resistance so

that by 1890 almost all the surviving Native Americans were confined to reservations (small areas given to them by the US government). More than a million Native Americans live on these reservations today.

THE AMERICAN CIVIL WAR

As America pursued its policy of expansion, tensions mounted between the industrialized states of the north, which had abandoned slavery, and the agricultural slave-owning states in the south. In 1854, the Republican Party was founded, largely in opposition to the extension of slavery, and in 1860, Abraham Lincoln, a well-known opponent of slavery, became president. Fearing that Lincoln would attempt to extend the abolition of slavery across the US, seven southern states split from the Union to form a Confederacy.

Hostilities started in 1861 when Confederate troops fired on Union forces at Fort Sumter in South Carolina. Four more states joined the rebel Confederates and war was declared. At first, the Confederates won victories led by such generals as 'Stonewall' Jackson. But the Confederates' advance in the north was halted after the Battle of Gettysburg in 1863, while in the west the Union gained control of the Mississippi River at the Battle of Vicksburg. Union forces had more men and supplies and gradually the south was worn down as Union general William Sherman captured Atlanta, Georgia, and marched to the sea.

The Confederate leader Robert E. Lee eventually surrendered to the Union's Lieutenant General, Ulysses S. Grant, at Appomattox in April 1865. It was one of America's most brutal wars with over 600,000 soldiers and an undetermined number of civilians killed during hostilities.

THE SLAVE TRADE AND ABOLITION MOVEMENT

Since the 1500s, Europeans had been capturing slaves from Africa and transporting them to plantations on European colonies in the Americas, but the practice increased dramatically during the eighteenth century so that several hundred thousand Africans were being transported across the Atlantic each year. By 1800 half the population of Brazil was of African origin, and by the mid nineteenth century an estimated 9.5 million Africans had been transported to the New World.

The slaves were exchanged for export goods and forced to work on European and then American plantations where they lived a life of suffering and toil, working long hours, frequently abused and beaten. More than a million slaves also died on their way to the New World due to the appalling conditions in which they were kept.

As awareness of the brutal realities of slavery grew,

people began to demand an end to it. In Britain, religious groups were at the forefront of the campaign, with Methodist preacher John Wesley publishing his influential anti-slavery pamphlet in 1774. In 1787, the Society of the Abolition of the Slave Trade was formed by William Wilberforce and Thomas Clarkson. However, in spite of support from Prime Minister William Pitt, an abolition bill was defeated in 1791. It wasn't until 1807 that the buying and selling of slaves was abolished in Britain and its empire, though slave ownership continued in British colonies. In 1833 slavery was abolished in all British colonies.

Thousands of slaves were freed by the British and strict measures to enforce the laws against the slave trade were implemented. However, thousands of slaves were still being exported from West Africa to America, Brazil and Cuba, where demand for cotton and sugar was high. In 1888 Brazil became the last South American country to abolish slavery.

In the US, most of the industrialized northern states had voluntarily abolished slavery by 1804. The cause of the abolitionists grew and as many as 100,000 slaves are thought to have escaped to the north from the southern states via the 'Underground Railroad', a network of abolitionist sympathizers who protected and hid fugitive slaves on their way north. In 1852, Harriet Beecher Stowe's novel *Uncle Tom's Cabin* sold in its millions, and its stark depiction of the evils of slavery turned abolitionism into a moral crusade.

After the American Civil War, Abraham Lincoln's Emancipation Proclamation of 1863 was finally put into practice and slavery was abolished across all US states in 1865. However, the legal practice of slavery in some countries, particularly in Africa and the Arab nations, continued into the twentieth century.

COLONIAL WARS

European empires were busy acquiring their dominions piecemeal and, as the century progressed, imperial nations were engaged in almost constant overseas conflict, as each empire struggled to expand and retain its territories in the face of either foreign aggression or internal mutiny. Here are some of the key conflicts that shaped the political boundaries of the globe and would have far-reaching consequences for the great conflicts of the next century.

The Opium Wars (1839–42 and 1856–60)

In the early nineteenth century, British traders were intent on opening up trade in China to foreigners and were illegally exporting opium from India to China, to exchange for the latter's teas and silks. To prevent this and protect their opium trade, the Chinese seized and destroyed over 20,000 chests of opium from British

IMPERIAL CHINA

At the time of the Opium Wars, China was governed by the Qing dynasty, a ruling elite led by Manchu emperors and successors to the Ming Dynasty. Powerful in the eighteenth century, the Qing dynasty thereafter weakened in authority, causing China to succumb to foreign intervention. The subsequent Opium Wars further weakened the emperor's control, and subsequent civil war and rebellion (including the Taiping Civil War of 1851–64) devastated the economy and cost tens (if not hundreds) of millions of lives. Defeat in the Sino-Japanese War (see page 144) and the Boxer Rising of 1900 precipitated attempts at imperial reform but further civil disorder ultimately led to the Chinese Revolution of 1911–2 and the end of imperial rule in China.

warehouses, whereupon the British sent a force of sixteen British warships which besieged Canton (Guangzhou) advanced to Tianjin, threatening the capital Peking (Beijing) and capturing Shanghai in 1842. The war ended with the Treaty of Nanjing in which Hong Kong was ceded to the British, and treaty ports set up in China that would be open to British trade.

The Second Opium War broke out when the Qing authorities (see opposite) refused demands to renegotiate more favourable terms to the Nanjing Treaty, and the French joined the British in launching a military attack on the Chinese. Beijing was overthrown and the Chinese finally agreed to the Treaty of Tianjin in 1860 which provided freedom of travel to European, American and Russian merchants and missionaries and opened ten further ports to western trade.

The Indian Mutiny (1857–8)

Since the 1600s, the East India Company had gained control of a large part of India, building up an army made of British and local soldiers (the Bengal army). The Indian Mutiny began when sepoys (Indian soldiers under British command) in the Bengal army refused to use cartridges greased with pig and cow fat (offensive to Muslims and Hindus respectively). The mutinies rapidly spread to Delhi and to most regiments of the Bengal army as well as to a large section of the civilian population. The major centres of rebellion were Delhi, Lucknow and Cawnpore (now Kanpur), where over 200 British women and children were massacred but for which the reprisals were equally savage.

In response, the British government transferred the

control of India from the East India Company to the Crown, managed by the India Office, a government department. Thereafter, a vast railway network was built, and as trade prospered India became a source of great wealth for Britain.

The Crimean War (1853–6)

The Crimean War was one of the bloodiest and shambolic wars in European history, in which as many as half of the 1.2 million soldiers who went out to fight lost their lives. It was fought by Russia against the Allied forces of Turkey, Britain, France and Piedmont and was caused by a long-running feud between the European powers over territories in the declining Ottoman Empire. War was triggered when Russian forces attacked a Turkish fleet, and Britain and France, anxious to limit the ambitions of the Russians and protect trade routes, joined with Turkey to fight against the Russians.

Ill-equipped and badly prepared, thousands of Allied troops succumbed to disease, though conditions improved with the intervention of Florence Nightingale ('The Lady with the Lamp') and her promotion of hygiene standards. The Allied forces eventually won and the Russians signed a peace treaty in 1856, but public opinion had already turned against the war as, for the first time, photographers such as Roger Fenton were able to show the realities of the conflict.

THE CHARGE OF THE LIGHT BRIGADE

The most notorious battle of the Crimean War took place at Balaklava in 1854 (famously depicted in Alfred, Lord Tennyson's poem of the same name). A misconstrued order from the army commander, Lord Raglan, led the British Light Horse Brigade, under the Earl of Cardigan, to charge the length of a narrow valley only to be ruthlessly bombarded by cannon and small-arms fire from the Russians above: 40 per cent of the Light Brigade perished.

The Franco-Prussian War (1870-1)

War between France and Prussia was provoked by the Prussian Chancellor Otto von Bismarck, who predicted that a victorious war would lead to the unification of Germany under Prussian leadership. Prussian forces, aided by a coalition of German states, advanced into France and defeated the French army at the Battle of Sedan, capturing the French Emperor Napoleon III. German forces later laid siege to Paris, during which its population rose in revolt. In January 1871, the German states proclaimed their union under the new Prussian

King William I. The war marked the end of the Second French Empire and the establishment of the Third French Republic, and the German Empire swiftly became the dominant power in Continental Europe. Alsace and Lorraine were also ceded to Germany, a deep source of resentment for France and a contributing factor to the First World War.

Japanese Colonial Wars

The First Sino-Japanese War (1894–5) was the result of a rivalry between China and Japan over the control of Korea (a former vassal state of China). Chinese forces were rapidly overwhelmed by the superior Japanese and the Chinese were forced to accept Korean independence and cede territories to Japan, including Taiwan.

The Russo-Japanese War (1904–5) broke out between Japan and Russia over control of Korea and Manchuria. A surprise Japanese attack on Russian warships led to the destruction of Russian troops on both land and sea. This humiliating defeat led to the Russian Revolution of 1905, a shift of power balance in the East, and the type of warfare, with protracted battles and extended fronts, characteristic of the First World War.

IMPERIAL JAPAN

Since 1192, Japan had been ruled by the shogun, hereditary military leaders who exercised power on behalf of their emperors. From the 1630s onwards, Japan had little contact with the outside world until the nineteenth century when foreign intervention began to weaken the authority of the Tokugawa shogunate. In 1853 and 1854 Commodore Matthew Perry of the US Navy visited Japan and agreed a treaty that opened two ports to US trade. Further treaties with other countries followed, and armed opposition in 1868 eventually succeeded in replacing the shogunate with the emperor Meiji Tennor (the Meiji Restoration). Thereafter, feudalism was dismantled and Japan was rapidly modernized and industrialized. Japan then embarked on a series of military conflicts.

CONFLICT AND A NEW WORLD ORDER

The twentieth century was characterized by massive military upheaval. Two world wars dissolved the colonial empires formed over the last two centuries, devastated nations and led to the loss of millions of lives. In the aftermath, the United Nations was formed to ensure peace and stability, but hostility prevailed between Western powers and the Soviet Union as both superpowers struggled for supremacy in the Cold War.

THE TRIPLE ENTENTE

By the start of the twentieth century, alliances between European powers were shifting. The Entente Cordiale, signed in 1904, formalized a 'friendly agreement' between France and Britain, both of whom had become increasingly isolated in the latter half of the nineteenth century. The two countries had clashed over colonial interests in Morocco, Egypt, western Africa and the Pacific. The Entente Cordiale settled overseas disputes and ensured that the two nations would not interfere in each other's empire-building.

A series of agreements with Russia, already an ally of France, then developed into the Triple Entente (which would form the basis of the Allied forces in the First World War). The Entente was partly a response to the growing threat of Germany, which had been united under the Prussian 'Iron Chancellor' Otto von Bismarck following the Franco-Prussian War (see page 143). Germany had formed the Triple Alliance in 1882 with Italy and Austria (later joined by the Ottoman Empire and Bulgaria), and had grown in military and industrial might in the later years of the nineteenth century. The new Kaiser William II was intent on making Germany a world power and in 1898 began an ambitious naval-building programme to challenge the maritime supremacy of Great Britain. Helmuth von Moltke, Germany's bellicose Chief of General Staff, sued for war 'the sooner the better'. A fierce arms race between the two countries ensued, both building powerful battleships. As the two nations fought for dominance on the sea, other European powers looked to modernize their armed forces as tension mounted.

THE FIRST WORLD WAR

In Sarajevo on 28 June 1914, a young Bosnian Serb assassinated Archduke Franz Ferdinand, heir to the Austrian throne, for radical nationalist reasons. In retaliation, Austria-Hungary declared war on Serbia and one by one, through various entangling allegiances, all the other major European powers were drawn into the crisis. Russia supported Serbia, assembling forces along its Austrian and German borders, causing Germany to declare war on Russia and its ally, France, in response. Germany, implementing its plan for a pre-emptive attack on France, invaded Belgium on 3 August 1914, resulting in Britain declaring war on Germany on 4 August due to its obligation to protect Belgian neutrality. The 'war to end all wars' was one of the deadliest conflicts in history, with the mobilization of 70 million personnel and over 30 million military and civilian casualties (including 8.5 million war dead).

The Western Front
The Germans pushed back British forces in Belgium and crossed into north-west France, beginning an attack and counter-attack between the Germans and the Allied forces as the two sides scrambled to the north – 'the race for the sea'. By the end of the year both sides had dug hundreds of miles of defensive trenches from the border of Switzerland to the Belgian coast. Despite a series of major offensives, the line moved no more than 10 miles either way in the next three years, but by the end of the war 6,250 miles of trenches had been dug along the Western Front.

The key battles on the Western Front were fought at Ypres, Verdun and the Somme. There were three major

WOMEN'S SUFFRAGE

Political reform in the nineteenth century had expanded the British electorate, but women were still unable to vote or stand for election. In 1897, the National Union of Women's Suffrage Societies, the 'Suffragists', began lobbying for universal suffrage and in 1903 Emmeline Pankhurst set up the more militant Women's Social and Political Union (the 'Suffragettes'). Campaigns on both sides of the debate were quieter during the war, but in 1918 property-owning women over thirty were granted the vote and by 1928 they could vote on equal terms with men. New Zealand was the first country to grant women the vote in 1893, though the US didn't follow until 1920. The last European country to grant equal voting rights for women was Switzerland in 1971.

battles for the strategically situated city of Ypres between 1914 and 1917, with the third (known as the Battle of Passchendaele) resulting in over half a million casualties, with only a few miles of ground gained by the Allies. Despite a massive attack by the Germans on the French city of Verdun on 21 February 1916, the French forced them back. Later that year, the British and French forces tried to break through the German lines north of the River Somme leading to one of the bloodiest battles ever recorded, with over 1.5 million casualties. Early mistakes cost the British dearly, and Allied forces had only managed to advance 6 miles into German-held territory by the end of the battle in November 1916.

The Eastern Front and Other Theatres of War

On the Eastern Front, Russia unsuccessfully attempted to invade the German province of East Prussia in 1914, then had better luck holding the Austrian province of Galicia before being pushed back by Austro-Hungarian and German armies, losing Poland to the Germans in August 1915.

In the Middle East, the Ottoman Empire's decision to ally itself with the Central Powers led to Britain sending an Anglo-Indian force to Mesopotamia (now part of Iraq) to protect its crucial oil supply, causing the Ottoman Turks to attack Suez in 1915 in an unsuccessful retaliation. After failed Allied naval attacks on the strategically important Ottoman-controlled Dardanelles Strait (in order to threaten the Turkish capital of Constantinople), British, French, Australian and New Zealand troops invaded Turkey from the sea twice in 1915, landing on the Gallipoli Peninsula. However, they were forced to retreat in 1916 and as a result of these defeats the Allies redoubled their presence in the Middle East, finally breaking through the Ottoman lines at Gaza in October 1917. A force of British, New Zealand and Australian troops occupied Jerusalem in December, followed by Damascus and Aleppo. Meanwhile the Mesopotamian campaign had culminated in the capture of Baghdad in March 1917. By the end of October 1918, the Ottoman Empire had signed an armistice.

In Africa, meanwhile, with 3 million Commonwealth soldiers coming to Britain's aid in the war, it is unsurprising that they and France attempted to expand their empires by using forces from their territories to target German colonies in western Africa, capturing Togoland in 1914 and Kamerun (now Cameroon) in 1916. German South-West Africa fell in 1915. However, a vast force of British, African and Indian troops been tied up in German East Africa by a small force of Germans and Africans, which only surrendered two weeks after the Armistice had been signed.

The Italians joined the Allies in 1915, though due to poor preparation suffered huge casualties in eleven disastrous attacks on its mountainous borders with Austria, and were finally scattered before a combined Austro-Hungarian and German attack at Caporetto in late 1917. The remaining Italian force, strengthened by Allied reinforcements after their retreat, took revenge at the Battles of the Piave River and Vittorio Veneto,

THE DECLINE OF THE OTTOMAN EMPIRE

By the early twentieth century, the Ottoman Empire was in terminal decline due in part to the expansion of western European empires, and the discovery of new trade routes. By the end of the Balkan Wars in 1913, the Ottomans had lost most of their European and North African territories. They lost more provinces in Arabia and Greece during the First World War and, in 1922, the caliphate was abolished and the Republic of Turkey declared.

taking half a million Austrian prisoners and restoring the pre-war border.

At sea, despite massive pre-war naval building, the only major battle, fought in 1916 near Jutland (Denmark), was inconclusive. However, Germany's concentration on submarine warfare, with its fleet of U-boats targeting Allied merchant and troop ships, caused many problems for the Allies, and was certainly a contributing factor – particularly after the sinking of the *Lusitania* passenger ship in 1915 – to America's crucial decision to join the war in 1917.

The End of the War

In spring 1918, the Germans launched a massive campaign on the Western Front using troops transferred from the Eastern Front following a treaty with Russia (see page 156). However, with the help of the Americans, the Allied line held and by the time the Allies counter-attacked and pierced the previously impregnable 'Hindenburg Line', the worn-out German army was forced to retreat. On 7 November 1918 Germany sued for peace and on 11 November, in a railway carriage in Compiègne, the Armistice was signed.

Versailles and Other Treaties

The Treaty of Versailles concluded peace terms between the Allied Forces and Germany and was one of the main post-war settlements of 1919–23. The talks were dominated by the US, Britain and France. Germany was made to accept sole responsibility for the war. She was to pay reparations to the Allies for damage caused in the war and her armed forces were to be strictly limited. All German colonial possessions were given up, along with territories in Europe, including ceding Alsace-Lorraine to France and west Prussia to the restored nation Poland. The League of Nations was set up as a peacekeeping organization and Germany was not allowed to become a member until it had shown itself to be a peaceful country, which it did in 1926.

Other treaties were signed at the Paris Peace Conference with Bulgaria, Austro-Hungary and Turkey. Bulgaria was forced to pay reparations, accept limits to its army and cede territory to Romania, Greece and Yugoslavia. The Habsburg Empire of Austro-Hungary was effectively dismantled, as Poland and the newly created Czechoslovakia became independent states and all occupied territories were surrendered, and its navy dismantled. The Ottoman Empire was divided up under the Treaty of Sèvres and then again, after a war with Greece, at Lausanne in 1923; the Republic of Turkey retained some of its Greek territory, but ceded Syria under a French League of Nations mandate and Iraq, Palestine and Jordan under a British mandate, while other territories were given up to Greece and Italy and the Dardanelles was overseen by the League of Nations.

THE RUSSIAN REVOLUTIONS

When it entered the First World War, Russia was in a state of crisis as social unrest and disorder had swept through the country. Heavy taxation had brought mounting distress to the poor and Russia's involvement and eventual defeat in its war with Japan aggravated discontent (see page 144).

TSAR NICHOLAS II (1868–1917)

Overshadowed by his more charismatic and forceful father Alexander III, Nicholas was a weak and wavering tsar subject to the will of the advisers around him. In spite of his weakness, or because of it, the last of the Romanov tsars clung to the idea of his supreme right to rule – and was out of touch with the mood of the people. Nicholas was forced to abdicate in 1917 following the February Revolution (see page 156) and he and his family were finally shot by the Bolsheviks in 1918.

The Revolution of 1905

On 9 January 1905, later called Bloody Sunday, peaceful demonstrators demanding higher wages and shorter hours were fired on by government troops in St Petersburg: 150 people were killed and the tsar was further discredited. The result was the Revolution of 1905, with strikes across the country and mutinies within the armed forces. Nicholas II was forced to grant a Constitution providing for a Duma (Parliament). However, disorder and strikes continued as Russia entered the First World War, struggling to supply its troops at the front and suffering huge casualties (over 5 million men by 1917).

The February Revolution

In February 1917, after a winter of poverty and hunger, there were renewed disturbances in St Petersburg (now Petrograd) in which the troops ordered to fire on striking protesters refused and instead joined the uprising, which culminated with the tsar's abdication on 2 March and the formation of the Russian Provisional Government.

The October Revolution and Civil War

In the October Revolution of 1917, Vladimir Lenin's Bolshevik Party seized power. The Bolsheviks took over government entirely, promising 'peace, bread and land' to the Russian people. The Germans offered the first of these, but with the punitive terms of the Treaty of Brest-Litovsk, which the Bolsheviks signed in March 1918. It was one of the most brutal treaties in history, forcing Russia to cede 60 million people, almost a third of its agricultural land and over three-quarters of its coal reserves. Civil war ensued between the Reds (the Bolsheviks) and the Whites (the more conservative anti-Bolshevik Russians). The Russian Communist Party, as the Bolsheviks called themselves from 1918, gained supremacy and established the Soviet Union in 1922.

During the civil war Lenin oversaw practices of state

KEY TERMS OF COMMUNISM

Communism: A political system in which there is shared ownership of property and whose ideal is of a classless society, as laid out in Marx and Engels's *Communist Manifesto* of 1848.

Marxism: The economic theory derived from the doctrines of Friedrich Engels and Karl Marx, which states that the economy is at the root of all social oppression. In Marx's model, capitalism is doomed to failure as revolution of the proletariat is inevitable.

Socialism: Economic theory favouring cooperation as opposed to capitalist competition. Early socialists didn't believe in armed revolution and their view of politics was directly challenged by Marx. Lenin defined socialism as the transitional stage between capitalism and Communism

terror in the form of torture and summary execution of anyone opposed to the revolution. All industry was placed under state control and any nonconformity with Bolshevism treated as counter-revolutionary. In 1918 Lenin was shot twice. He seemingly recovered but suffered subsequent strokes. The civil war was over by 1920 but the economy was in a state of collapse. Lenin allowed small-scale industries to be denationalized but retained a vice-like grip on political dissent.

Joseph Vissarionovich joined the Bolsheviks under Lenin and in 1913 adopted the name 'Stalin' ('man of steel'). He became the Communist Party's general secretary and, following Lenin's death in 1924, sidelined Leon Trotsky, who had helped Lenin organize the October Revolution, to become the uncontested leader by 1927. In the following year he launched programmes to expand and collectivize farming and rapidly develop industry. Millions of peasants who resisted were shot or sent to labour camps while others died from famine as the government seized grain from producers. Stalin eliminated political opposition in the Great Purges in 1935–8 as the intelligentsia, members of the Party, army officers and millions of others were executed or sent to Gulag labour camps.

The Anglo-Irish Conflict

The issue of Home Rule in Ireland had long been fiercely debated in government (see page 128). In 1914, Prime Minister Asquith finally passed the Home Rule Act, which reinstated a limited form of self-government in Ireland, but crucially held back application of this law until after the First World War. However, many Protestants in the north-east of Ireland were opposed to southern Catholic-dominated rule. Unionists in Ulster formed the Ulster Volunteers and prepared to seize power as soon as the Act came into effect: Ireland was on the brink of civil war.

The 1916 Easter Rising

Radical republican groups, led by the Irish Republican Brotherhood (IRB) and supported by the Irish National Volunteers, saw Britain's preoccupation with the war as the perfect time to stage an uprising. On Easter Monday 1916, rebels seized the General Post Office in Dublin and proclaimed an Irish Republic. After six days of fighting, the rebellion was crushed, sixteen of its leaders executed and over 2,000 men and women imprisoned. While the rising itself failed, the reprisals served to radicalize opinion, turning many moderates against the British and laying the foundations for the Irish War of Independence.

The Establishment of the Irish Free State

Following Britain's heavy handling of the Easter Rising, Irish voters overwhelmingly supported the separatist political party Sinn Fein in elections two years later. Sinn Fein's military arm, the IRA (Irish Republican Army) under Michael Collins, mounted a savage guerrilla war against the British Army and paramilitary forces (the Black and Tans and the Auxiliaries), called the Irish War of Independence (1919–21), in which atrocities were committed by both sides.

In December 1921, Prime Minister Lloyd George negotiated an Anglo-Irish Treaty that gave separate dominion status to Ireland as an 'Irish Free State', with the exception of six counties in Ulster that formed Northern Ireland. Hard-line nationalists, who believed that all of Ireland should be a republic, remained opposed to the treaty. A two-year civil war (1922–3) between rival republican factions spread throughout the country and led to the death of Michael Collins. Thereafter, aspects of the treaty were gradually dismantled until the south declared itself a republic in all but name in the constitution of 1937. In 1948 this declaration was made official, with Britain formally acknowledging the Republic of Eire in 1949.

THE RISE OF ITALIAN FASCISM

Benito Mussolini (who had been a primary school teacher before becoming the dictator of Italy) founded a Fascist force in 1919. Mussolini had been a radical socialist, but he turned away from this, seeing Fascism as an anti-socialist, anti-capitalist movement. Mussolini became prime minister in 1922 and assumed the title *Il Duce*, 'the leader'.

THE ABYSSINIA CRISIS (1935)

The Abyssinia Crisis was a diplomatic crisis resulting from Italy's invasion of Abyssinia (now Ethiopia) in 1935. The weakness of the League of Nations was exposed when it was unable either to control Italy or to protect Ethiopia, both member states. The war resulted in the military occupation of Ethiopia, the exile of its emperor Haile Selassie and the annexation of Ethiopia into the newly created colony of Italian East Africa. It wasn't until the Second World War that British troops evicted the Italians from Ethiopia (as well as Eritrea and Somalia).

Mussolini's nationalist ideas spread across Europe, inspiring Hitler's vision of the German Reich and informing the nationalist political ideals of General Franco during the Spanish Civil War (see page 162).

Unlike Hitler, Mussolini was hindered by a dominant elite, and a monarch. Though he pursued an aggressive foreign policy during the Abyssinia Crisis (see above) and in the Second World War as a German ally, both wars proved unpopular and he was deposed in 1943. Italy signed an armistice with the Allies in the same year, and joined in the fight against Germany. Mussolini fled into exile and was shot by Italian partisans in 1945.

THE SPANISH CIVIL WAR

The Spanish Civil War began with a military coup in 1936 against the socialist Republican government of Spain; it was led by a group of right-wing army generals, fearful of the reforms that the government was planning. The country was divided with the Nationalist rebels gaining control of much of the north. The forces were also split, but most of the army, navy and air force remained loyal to the Republicans.

However, the intervention of Nazi Germany and Fascist Italy on the side of the Nationalists, swayed the balance. The Republican government was aided by the Soviet Union as well as thousands of individual volunteers from Europe and the US. Picasso's painting *Guernica* famously depicts the bombing of the town of the same name by Nationalist forces in 1937, but both sides were guilty of brutality.

By December 1938 the Nationalists had forced the Republican armies north towards France and on 5 March the Republican government was forced into exile. The war ended in April 1939 with the victory of the Nationalists and the founding of a Fascist dictatorship under General Franco that lasted until his death in 1975.

Hitler and Nazi Germany

Austrian born, Adolf Hitler had fought and been wounded in the First World War and was profoundly affected by Germany's defeat and the humiliating terms of the Treaty of Versailles. One of many disaffected agitators against Germany's post-war government, he swiftly became leader of a small nationalist party, which became the National Socialist German Workers' Party or Nazi Party in 1922. After the Munich 'beer-hall putsch' of 1923, when he and others attempted to seize power in Bavaria, Hitler was imprisoned. He used this time to compose his political manifesto *Mein Kampf* (*My Struggle*).

The Great Depression (1929–39), following the Wall Street Crash, resulted in 6 million Germans unemployed, thus helping to boost the popularity of the nationalist Nazi Party, as Hitler promised to restore national pride and create jobs and railed against the Treaty of Versailles, which had crippled the country.

In 1933, Hitler was Chancellor and swiftly established a one-party dictatorship, eliminating his rivals in the 'Night of the Long Knives'. Following President Paul von Hindenburg's death a year later, Hitler appointed himself president and Führer (leader) of the German Reich (state), and thereafter assumed total control of the country.

With his authority at home unchallenged, Hitler began rearmament in contravention of the Treaty of Versailles, reoccupying the Rhineland in 1936, annexing Austria in 1938 and beginning the piecemeal occupation of Czechoslovakia. Desparate to avoid war, Britain and France had adopted a policy of appeasement towards Hitler, with Prime Minister Neville Chamberlain declaring 'peace in our time' following his return from the Munich Conference in 1938. But, as German tanks advanced into the rest of Czechoslovakia, Britain abandoned its policy of appeasement and promised to defend Poland should Hitler invade it.

THE SECOND WORLD WAR

In the early hours of 1 September 1939, Germany launched the blitzkrieg ('lightning war': a combined attack of fast-moving tanks, troops and dive-bombers), its tanks rolling into Poland from the west, while Soviet Russian forces invaded from the east, the result of a secret Nazi–Soviet pact agreed in August. Soon after, Britain and France declared war on Germany. For a few months, there followed a 'Phoney War' in which little happened as Hitler regrouped his forces. This came to an end in April 1940 when Germany invaded Denmark and then Norway, followed by Holland and Belgium. As these countries fell, Hitler advanced into France, leading to the Allies suffering one of the worst military disasters of the war.

The War on Land

By 24 May 1940, thousands of Allied troops had been trapped on the beaches around Dunkirk, having been cut off by a German advance in northern France. Prime Minister Winston Churchill, who had recently succeeded the ineffectual Chamberlain, ordered an emergency evacuation: in nine days, the Royal Navy, now aided by hundreds of civilian craft, carried some 338,000 British and French troops back to the UK. Three weeks after the evacuation of Dunkirk, France surrendered to the Germans. General Charles de Gaulle escaped to Britain and established the Free French Forces and a French government-in-exile. The Nazis occupied the north and west of France, while a pro-German puppet government was installed under Marshal Petain at Vichy, in the so-called 'free zone'. From 1942, following the Allied invasions of Vichy French territories in North Africa, German forces occupied all of France, enforcing Nazi laws, with Vichy collaboration, and deporting French Jews and resistance workers to Germany, where most died in the camps.

In June 1941, Hitler advanced into Russia, towards the oilfields of the Caucasus. After huge territorial gain, the main German advance was barred by the Soviet defence of Stalingrad in south-western Russia. The Germans reached the centre, but the massive Soviet counter-attack trapped them in the city. The German commander-in-chief surrendered in January 1943. With as many as 2 million military and civilian casualties on both sides, the disastrous German defeat halted their advance into Russia and marked a major turning point in the war.

Another turning point for the Allies occurred in late 1942 at El Alamein on the Egyptian coast. General Montgomery's British forces (aided by troops from South Africa, New Zealand and Australia, as well as Free French and Greek forces) secured a decisive victory and prevented German Field Marshal Rommel's forces from occupying Egypt and advancing towards the Suez Canal.

THE HOLOCAUST

Nazi ideology centred on a belief in the superiority of the German race and held that Germany could achieve domination only by purging the nation of 'weak groups', which included Jews, gypsies, Communists and even the mentally disabled. Hitler targeted Jews in particular and, on coming to power in 1933, he began to exclude them from German society. The Nuremberg Laws of 1935 deprived Jews of citizenship; by 1937 Jewish businesses were being confiscated and anti-Semitic propaganda circulated.

In the *Kristallnacht* ('Crystal Night', from the broken glass that lay on the streets) of 9 November 1938, synagogues were burnt down and Jewish shops looted. Many Jews fled Germany and Austria and moved abroad (often forced to leave their property and assets to be seized by the Nazis). As the Nazis occupied other European countries the persecutions spread, with forced-labour concentration camps and mass shootings.

The extermination camps provided the 'final solution' to the Jewish 'problem', as finalized by leading Nazis at Wannsee, Berlin in early 1942. Six 'extermination' camps were built in Poland, equipped with gas chambers. Jews were transported to these camps from all over Nazi-occupied Europe; nearly 6 million Jews were killed, along with Soviet, Polish and other POWs, political and religious opponents, captured enemy agents, people with disabilities and other minority groups.

The War at Sea

The Battle of the Atlantic was a struggle kept up throughout the war between German and Allied forces for domination of the shipping routes to Britain. German U-boats (submarines) were the main weapon of attack; they claimed an average of ninety-six ships per month in 1942. However, by 1943, better radar and intelligence gleaned through the British decryption of the German cipher machine, Enigma, enabled Britain to re-route convoys away from U-boat 'wolf packs'. Enigma intelligence was also crucial to Allied victories in North Africa, Italy and Normandy.

Meanwhile, the Japanese had set their sights upon unprotected British, French and Dutch colonial possessions in Asia and the Pacific. On 7 December 1941 they attacked the US Pacific Fleet's base at Pearl Harbor, Hawaii, sinking several ships, thereby provoking the US to join the war on the side of the Allies. (Churchill said he slept 'the sleep of the saved' that night.)

Aided by decrypted communication, the American fleet ambushed and defeated the Japanese fleet at the Battle of the Coral Sea in May 1942 and the Battle of Midway the following month. Thereafter, the US Navy, with British, Australian and other forces in support, ultimately succeeded in defeating Japanese naval power in the Pacific, leading to the eventual recapture of several Japanese-occupied territories through a series of amphibious operations, including the assaults on Iwo Jima, Guadalcanal and Okinawa.

SECOND SINO-JAPANESE WAR (1937–45)

War broke out once more in the Far East as China attempted to seize back territory that the Japanese had begun occupying from 1931. Stalemate ensued and Japanese forces were diverted to the Second World War – its eventual defeat by the Americans resulted in the restoration of its Chinese territories.

The War in the Air

After the fall of France, Hitler launched a bombing offensive against Britain as a prelude to invasion, attacking shipping and ports, then airfield and communication centres in southern England. However, the Germans met significant resistance from the Royal Air Force during the Battle of Britain (August–October 1940) and suffered heavy losses from fighter aircraft and ground defences, crucially assisted by the radar, then highly secret. On 12 October Hitler postponed and ultimately abandoned his invasion of Britain, codenamed 'Operation Sea Lion'.

Nevertheless, between September 1940 and May 1941, the sustained bombing of British cities, known as the Blitz, continued, with the intended goal of demoralizing

Britain into surrender. Over the course of the Blitz, 2 million buildings were seriously damaged or destroyed and 60,000 civilians killed.

The sustained American and British strategic bombing of Germany proved even more devastating. Between May 1942 and July 1945 German factories and military zones were targeted, as well as towns and cities, notably Hamburg, Dresden and Berlin. An estimated 750,000 to 1 million German civilians were killed in total.

D-Day Landings and Victory in Europe

By 1944, the German hold on Europe was weakening and the Allied invasion of Normandy was put in hand; its aim to liberate western Europe and also to take the pressure off Soviet forces fighting on the Eastern Front. On 6 June 1944, the Germans were caught off-guard as 156,000 men landed on five Normandy beaches. Allied forces eventually broke through the German defences and by 25 August the Allies had liberated Paris.

Thereafter, the Allies pushed through Europe, despite heavy casualties during the Battle of the Bulge in the Ardennes and at Arnhem in Holland. In March 1945, they crossed the Rhine and entered Germany, and in April linked up with the advancing Soviet Army. Realizing he was defeated, Hitler shot himself on 30 April. On 8 May 1945 the Allies accepted Germany's unconditional surrender and declared Victory in Europe.

The End of the War

In July and August 1945, following the German surrender the leaders of the 'big three' Allied nations of Russia, the US and Britain met at the Potsdam Conference. Stalin, Truman (who had succeeded Roosevelt) and Churchill (later replaced by Clement Attlee) agreed on the terms of Germany's reparations and its division into four Allied occupation zones.

Meanwhile, the defeat of the Japanese in India and Burma by British and Commonwealth forces, the success of the American amphibious assaults

Allied Division of Germany in 1945

on Japanese-controlled territory and the heavy strategic bombing of Japan by the US culminated in atomic bombs being dropped on Hiroshima and Nagasaki on 6 and 9 August; 140,000 Japanese civilians died immediately, but many others later perished or suffered from radiation poisoning. On 2 September 1945, the Japanese surrendered and the Second World War was over. Over 50 million lives had been lost during the war.

THE UNITED NATIONS

The United Nations (UN) was set up in 1945 as a successor to the failed League of Nations with the aim of ensuring peace, security and cooperation among the nations of the world. In 1942, twenty-six Allied nations signed the Declaration of the United Nations and pledged to continue fighting together against Nazi Germany and the Axis powers. President Franklin D. Roosevelt had decided America should take the lead and, for this reason, the first United Nations Organization meeting took place in San Francisco on 25 April 1945. In June 1946, fifty member nations signed the United Nations' Charter and headquarters were set up in New York. The UN grew rapidly as former colonial territories gained independence and applied for membership and in 2015 has 193 members.

The Creation of Israel

In 1947, UN leaders voted that Palestine should be divided up into a Jewish state and an Arab state, with Jerusalem under UN governance. Palestine had been under a British mandate since the end of the First World War and Britain formally established the Zionist Jewish Agency to represent Jewish interests in the region in 1929. However, the Arab states rejected partition and the newly formed Zionist government declared an independent state of Israel. Arab-Israeli wars over

THE PARTITION OF INDIA (1947)

Indian nationalism had gained momentum during the nineteenth century, reaching a turning point with the Indian Mutiny of 1857 (see page 141). Unrest continued into the twentieth century, and Gandhi led a peaceful protest movement for Indian independence after the First World War. The massacre of nationalist demonstrators by British troops at Amritsar in 1919 further intensified anti-British sentiment. Tensions also escalated between Hindus and the Muslim minority, leading the Muslim League, formed in 1906, to demand a separate homeland for Muslims. India was granted independence from Britain in 1947 and divided into two states: India and the Muslim state of Pakistan. Partition marked the end of the British Empire, but it also displaced millions of people, and led to the deaths of hundreds of thousands in the ensuing unrest between Hindus and Muslims.

territories continued over the following decades, as Israel enlarged its territories, and conflict in the region continues to the present day.

THE COLD WAR

At the wartime summit meetings of Yalta and Potsdam serious tensions had emerged between America and Britain and the Soviet Union over the future of Germany and Eastern Europe. America especially feared the spread of Soviet power and Communism – a fear intensified when, as well as its annexed territories, the Soviet Union went on to set up satellite republics in Poland (despite having promised to honour free and fair elections), Czechoslovakia and Hungary, thus extending the Eastern bloc of Soviet-controlled states even further. The Soviet blockade of Berlin in 1948 (during which supplies had to be airlifted into the city by British and American planes), and the eventual division of Germany between east and west further soured relationships.

Over the next few decades, the arms race maintained tension between the superpowers at a high level, as the US and Russia rushed to develop nuclear weapons. The Berlin Wall was constructed in 1961 to prevent mass defection of Communist East Germans over to the West, but the darkest moment in the Cold War was the Cuban Missile Crisis in 1962. The world held its breath for a week as the US successfully faced off the Soviet Union's ambition to base nuclear missiles in Cuba. Tension also intensified in the 1980s when President Ronald Reagan launched the development of the Strategic Defense

NATO

The North Atlantic Treaty Organization (NATO) was formed in 1949 as a military alliance between western European countries, the US and Canada originally against the perceived threat of Soviet aggression. With their headquarters in Brussels, twelve member states agreed that 'an armed attack against one or more of them in Europe or North America shall be considered an attack upon them all'. Another sixteen nations have since joined, including countries from the former Eastern bloc. To counter NATO, in 1955 the Soviet Union formed its own alliance – the Warsaw Pact – with countries of Eastern Europe.

Initiative (or Star Wars), a system designed to destroy any missiles aimed at the US.

Because neither power actually wanted a nuclear Armageddon, the US and Russia used proxy conflicts to advance their global influence, with Russia sending troops to support Communist rule in Afghanistan, Hungary, Czechoslovakia and East Germany, while the US helped to overthrow the Communist government in

Guatemala, supported an invasion of Cuba and invaded the Dominican Republic and Grenada. The US was particularly concerned about the 'domino effect' of states falling to communism in South East Asia and became involved in two costly and largely unsuccessful wars.

Korean War (1950–3)

At the end of the Second World War, Korea was divided into the Soviet-occupied North and US-occupied South. The respective occupying forces withdrew in 1949 and in 1950 North Korea invaded South Korea. Fearing the spread of communism in South East Asia, the US and sixteen other UN member-states sent forces under the command of General MacArthur to aid the South while Chinese troops fought on behalf of the North. By June 1951 there was a stalemate and in 1953 an armistice was signed, reinstating the original boundaries.

Vietnam War (1965–75)

Vietnam was also divided into two states by the Treaty of Geneva in 1954: North Vietnam under the communist government of Ho Chi Minh and South Vietnam under a government that was friendly to the West. In 1961, the US began to send increased military aid to South Vietnam to help it remove the Vietcong, a Communist guerrilla movement backed by the North who had been fighting to overthrow the government of South Vietnam. The US made direct intervention in 1964 following claims that North Vietnamese forces had attacked a US spy ship in the area.

By 1967 there were 500,000 US troops in Vietnam fighting the Vietcong. In January 1968, the Communists launched the Tet Offensive, which was eventually driven back. But as US casualties grew, it became clear that they could not win the war. Mounting costs and opposition to the war at home eventually led President Richard Nixon to pull out of Vietnam and in 1973 a ceasefire was agreed (though fighting continued). In 1975 North Vietnam and the Vietcong conquered South Vietnam and united it under Communism: a humiliating defeat for the US superpower. Millions of Vietnamese died in the war.

THE END OF THE COMMUNIST ERA

As the Cold War rumbled on, opposition to the Communist regime in the Eastern bloc gained momentum, first in Poland and then in Hungary in 1956, where an uprising was brutally repressed and a hard-line communist government established. In 1968, new leader Alexander Dubček tried to reform the Stalinist state of Czechoslovakia, although he was eventually removed and the country remained under Soviet control.

The advent of Mikhail Gorbachev as Soviet leader in 1985 signalled the beginning of liberalization. Gorbachev launched a series of policies designed to revive an ailing state through perestroika (a restructuring of the economy) and glasnost (openness to new ideas and freedom of speech). Relations between Moscow and Washington improved as Gorbachev directed Soviet resources away from the arms race and towards reviving the economy. In 1987, the Intermediate Range Nuclear Forces Treaty limited US and Soviet nuclear arsenals.

As part of his new economic policy, Gorbachev made it clear in 1988 that Soviet forces would no longer crush dissent in communist regimes. Both Hungary and Poland took advantage of this, with multi-party elections, followed by the establishment of the non-Communist Solidarity Party in Poland, led by Lech Walesa. Czechoslovakia, Bulgaria and Romania removed their communist governments, and in East Germany, a tidal wave of street protests led to the fall of the Berlin Wall and the eventual reunification of Germany in 1990.

The collapse of communism in the Eastern bloc accelerated as fifteen Soviet republics declared independence from the Union by 1991. In August 1991 a group of hard-line Communists staged a coup against Gorbachev. Boris Yeltsin, then the leader of a key industrial area of Russia, put the coup down, and the Communist Party was banned. Gorbachev resigned

THE LAST GREAT COMMUNIST STATE

After the fall of Communist Russia, the People's Republic of China, established by Chairman Mao Zedong in 1949, became the last great global Communist power. After the death of Mao in 1979 a programme of economic liberalism was instated, developing China into the third largest economy in the world, after Japan and the US. Any signs of rebellion against the communist government have in the past been dealt with swiftly and ruthlessly. When in 1989 peaceful pro-democracy protesters gathered in Tiananmen Square in Beijing, government troops fired on the demonstrators, leading to the deaths of an estimated 2,000 people.

on Christmas Day 1991, the Soviet Union was dissolved and Yeltsin became leader of an independent Russia – his official title being President of the Russian Federation. Communism had collapsed, leading many to declare that the Cold War was also at an end.

TIMELINE

*c.*5000–2000 BC Sumer civilization in Southern Mesopotamia

*c.*3200 BC Ancient Egypt emerges in Nile Valley

*c.*3000 BC Minoan civilization forms in Crete

*c.*2550–2470 BC Pyramids of Giza built in Egypt

*c.*2500–1500 BC Civilization flourishes along the Indus River

*c.*2000–605 BC Babylonian Empire thrives

*c.*1700–1200 BC Hittite Empire flourishes in the Mediterranean

*c.*1600 BC Shang dynasty emerges in China

1554–1075 BC New Kingdom of Ancient Egypt

*c.*1500 BC Olmec civilization emerges in South America

*c.*1450 BC Mycenaeans conquer the Minoans

*c.*1300 BC Assyrian Empire established

*c.*1180 BC Hittite Empire disintegrates

*c.*1046 BC Zhou dynasty comes to power in China

*c.*900 BC Celts appear in Gaul, Spain and British Isles

*c.*750 BC Greek city-states emerge

*c.*660 BC Assyrian Empire reaches its height

600 BC City of Rome is established

550 BC Cyrus the Great establishes the kingdom of Persia

539 BC Babylon becomes part of the Persian Empire

509 BC Rome becomes a republic

508 BC Athens established as a democracy

499–49 BC Persian Wars

486 BC Persian Empire reaches greatest extent

447–32 BC The Parthenon is built in Athens

338 BC Philip II of Macedonia conquers Greece

332–30 BC Alexander the Great occupies Egypt, then Persia

264–146 BC Punic Wars between Rome and Carthage

221 BC King of Qin forms first united empire in China

216 BC Battle of Cannae

146 BC Greek peninsula comes under Roman rule

31 BC Battle of Actium

30 BC Rome conquers Egypt

27 BC –AD 14 Augustus becomes first Roman emperor

AD 43 Emperor Claudius invades British Isles

AD 60 Revolt of Queen Boudicca

AD 97–117 Roman Empire reaches its greatest extent

AD 122 Construction of Hadrian's Wall begins

AD 286 Roman Empire divided into east and west

AD 330 Byzantine Empire established by Constantine I

AD c.370 The Huns invade south-eastern Europe

AD 378 Visigoths defeat and kill Roman Emperor Valens at Adrianople

AD c.400 Romans troops leave Britain

AD 410 Visigoths lay siege to Rome

AD 455 Hunnic Empire collapses

AD 476 Western Roman rule comes to end

AD 600 South and east of England become Anglo-Saxon kingdoms

AD 610 Prophet Muhammad founds Islam

AD 750-833 Golden Age of Muslim Empire under the Abbasid caliphate

AD 789 Viking raids of Britain begin

AD 800 Charlemagne crowned first Holy Roman Emperor

AD 871 Alfred the Great becomes king of the Anglo-Saxons

1054 Church in Constantinople breaks with Church in Rome

1066 Norman Conquest of England

1095–1291 The Crusades fought in the Holy Lands

1187 Saladin captures Jerusalem

1190–2 Richard I on Crusade

1215 Magna Carta signed by King John

1259 Treaty of Paris between England and France

c.1300 Ottoman Empire established

1337–1453 The Hundred Years Wars

1348 Black Death arrives in Europe

1381 Peasants' Revolt

1399 Richard II deposed by Henry IV

1415 English victory at Agincourt

1429 English defeated by Joan of Arc at Orléans

1453 Constantinople falls to the Ottoman Turks

1455–85 Wars of the Roses

1478 Spanish Inquisition set up by Pope Sixtus IV

1492 Christopher Columbus discovers the New World

1497 John Cabot lands on Newfoundland

1498 Vasco da Gama discovers sea route to East Indies

1499–1502 Amerigo Vespucci makes voyages to the Americas

1509 Henry VIII becomes king of England

1517 Martin Luther's ninety-five theses spark the Reformation

1520 Magellan Straits discovered

1534 Henry VIII breaks with Rome

1536–40 Dissolution of the Monasteries

1553 Mary I becomes queen of England

1558 England loses Calais to France

1558 Elizabeth I becomes queen of England

1559 The Act of Supremacy and Uniformity

1577–80 Francis Drake circumnavigates the world

1584 Virginia starts to be colonized

1588 English defeat of the Spanish Armada

1600 English East India Company given a royal charter

1602 Dutch East India Company founded

1603 James I becomes first joint monarch of Scotland and England

1605 Gunpowder Plot

1607 First English Colony at Jamestown, Virginia, established

1620 Pilgrim Fathers set sail on the *Mayflower*

1625 Charles I becomes king

1642–9 British Civil Wars

1649 Charles I executed

1649–60 Cromwell's Commonwealth

1660 Charles II restored to the throne

1670 Hudson's Bay Company founded

1688 The Glorious Revolution

1701–13 War of Spanish Succession

1707 Acts of Union

1769–70 Captain Cook sails to New Zealand and Australia

1775–83 American War of Independence

1778 First penal colony established in Australia

1789–99 French Revolution

1792–1815 French Revolutionary and Napoleonic Wars

1799 Consulate of Napoleon Bonaparte

1801 General Enclosure Act in Britain

1801 Second Act of Union results in the United Kingdom

1803 US purchases Louisiana from the French

1804 Napoleon becomes emperor

1812–5 War of 1812

1815 Napoleon defeated at Battle of Waterloo

1832 Great Reform Act

1833 Slavery abolished in British colonies

1837 Accession of Queen Victoria

1839–42 First Opium War

1845–51 Irish potato famine

1846 Britain cedes north-west America to US

1848 First Gold Rush in California

1853–6 Crimean War

1855 Livingstone discovers Victoria Falls

1856–60 Second Opium War

1857–8 Indian Mutiny

1861–5 American Civil War

1865 Slavery abolished in all US states

1870–1 Franco-Prussian War

1880–81 First Boer War

1882 Germany forms Triple Alliance with Austro-Hungary and Italy

1893 Women given the vote in New Zealand

1894–5 First Sino-Japanese War

1899–1902 Second Boer War

1901 Queen Victoria dies

1904 Anglo-French Entente Cordiale

1904–5 Russo-Japanese War

1905 Russian Revolution of 1905

1914 Irish Home Rule Act

1914–18 First World War

1914 First Battle of Ypres

1914 Russia defeated at Tannenberg

1915 Italians join Allies

1915–16 Dardanelles expedition and withdrawal from Gallipoli

1915 Second Battle of Ypres

1916 Easter Rising in Dublin

1916 Battle of Verdun

1916 Battle of the Somme

1917 Russian Revolutions

1917 Third Battle of Ypres (Passchendaele)

1918 Women granted the vote in UK

1918 Bolsheviks sue for peace with Germany

1918 Surrender of Ottoman Empire

1919 Treaty of Versailles, League of Nations established

1919 Mussolini founds Italian Fascist movement

1919–21 Irish War of Independence

1920 Women granted the vote in the US

1921 Irish Free State established

1922 The Soviet Union under Lenin is established

1922–3 Civil War in Ireland

1927 Stalin becomes Soviet leader

1933 Hitler comes to power in Germany

1935 Italy invades Abyssinia

1936–8 Stalin's Great Purges

1936–9 Spanish Civil War

1937–45 Second Sino-Japanese War

1939–45 Second World War

1940 Evacuation of Dunkirk

1940 France surrenders to Germany

1940 Battle of Britain

1940–1 The Blitz

1941 America and Russia enter the war

1942 'Final Solution' agreed by Nazis at Wannsee, Berlin

1942 Battle of the Coral Sea and Battle of Midway

1942–3 Battle of Stalingrad

1944 D-Day landings in Normandy

1945 Victory in Europe

1945 Atomic bombs dropped on Hiroshima and Nagasaki

1945 The United Nations established

1945 Postdam Conference and partition of Germany

1947 State of Israel created

1947 Partition of India

1948–9 Soviet blockade of Berlin

1948 Republic of Ireland (Eire) declared

1949 NATO formed

1949 People's Republic of China established by Chairman Mao

1950–3 Korean War

1955 Warsaw Pact signed

1956 Hungarian Uprising

1965–75 Vietnam War

1985 Mikhail Gorbachev becomes Soviet leader

1989 Collapse of Berlin Wall

1990 The reunification of Germany

1991 Soviet Union is dissolved and Boris Yeltsin becomes leader of independent Russia

SELECT BIBLIOGRAPHY

England under the Tudors by G. R. Elton (Methuen)

Eyewitness: World War I by Simon Adams (Dorling Kindersley)

History of the World by J. M. Roberts (Helicon)

Kings and Queens: The Millennium Series 1714–Present Day by John Guy
(Ticktock Publishing)

Oxford Dictionary of World History edited by Edmund Wright and Jonathan Law
(Oxford University Press)

The Dorling Kindersley History of the World by Plantagenet Somerset Fry
(Dorling Kindersley)

The New Penguin Dictionary of Modern History 1789–1945 edited by
Duncan Townson (Penguin)

The Oxford Illustrated History of Britain by Kenneth O Morgan
(Oxford University Press)

The Pelican History of Medieval Europe edited by Maurice Keen (Penguin Books)

The Usborne History of Britain by Ruth Brocklehurst (Usborne)

The Usborne Introduction to the Second World War edited by Paul Dowswell
(Usborne)